2016 Indie Author

State of the Union

Build Your Author Platform, Stay Up-to-Date, and
Sell More Books

Michael La Ronn

CONTENTS

Predictions for 2016

What's New in This Year's SOTU

Being an authorpreneur is tough, but it doesn't have to be that way.

The biggest problem indie authors face today is not a lack of information—it's too much of it. So much that it's hard to know what to use and what to ignore. Combine that with misinformation and it's no wonder why so many indie authors make critical mistakes.

This book will help you avoid many of those missteps.

Who I Am

I'm Michael La Ronn, author of over 20 books. I also co-host the *To Be Read Podcast*, which broadcasts weekly on YouTube, and am the founder of *Author Level Up*, a YouTube channel that publishes business, craft and marketing videos for authors every week.

I'm an authorpreneur, speaker, and consultant. I'm a part-time writer who has built a publishing business despite working a demanding job in the insurance industry, planning a wedding, and taking care of my infant daughter. Life always tried to get in the way, but I never let it stop me.

I made a promise to myself that I would stay in the shadows until I had at least 20 books, so that I could give myself plenty of time to figure out how to be a successful author. Nothing pisses me off more than bad advice, so you'll get no fluff or puffery from me.

But I wasn't always this confident. During my first year of publishing, I made every mistake in the book.

I followed advice blindly.

I hunted for shortcuts.

I spent a lot of money on "stuff" that didn't help my business.

I chased trends.

I didn't understand that it takes patience, humility, and insanity to be successful.

After spending an exorbitant amount of money on a marketing campaign that produced less than a 1% return, I swore that I would never make that mistake again.

I devoted myself to becoming a knowledgeable industry professional. I followed the major blogs and podcasts, I read all the recommended writing books, and I connected with successful authors.

I did this for myself, but I soon realized that I wasn't the only author out there who wanted to be a smarter authorpreneur but didn't know how to filter through all the noise.

That's why I created the *Indie Author State of the Union*: To share a snapshot of the publishing industry with authors so they can make better business decisions.

What You'll Find in This Book

You'll learn the biggest publishing industry news that affects indie authors. You'll also discover the best books, podcasts and courses released in the last calendar year. Almost every indie author will find something unexpected and useful in this book.

Reading this book will make you a smarter authorpreneur so you can operate at your very best.

Even better, I completely redesigned the book this year from the ground up.

* Every article in this book is actionable. You'll be able to apply almost every tip to your situation immediately. When I was writing this collection, I asked two questions about everything I encountered: Do authors need to know it, and if so, can they apply it? Only the most practical advice made it into these pages.

* The book is divided into themed sections: Ebook retailers, traditional

publishing, libraries, copyright/legal, marketing, etc. You can quickly scan the book and jump to the sections you're most interested in.

* The news is objective as possible, but I'll be commenting on it more this year. Readers told me that they wanted to hear my opinions, so for better or worse, they're going to get it! However, the reporting is still objective. I keep my opinions confined to the end of each article, and you can refer to the Sources section to check out all my sources for yourself.

So without further ado, welcome to the *Indie Author State of the Union*. I had a blast writing this book. It's awesome to have you here.

I wish you all the best in your author career, and I hope this is the most helpful book you'll read all year.

Book Retailers

One of my favorite parts of the *Indie Author State of the Union* is following book retailers.

Keeping track of Amazon, Barnes & Noble, Kobo, etc. is a very smart thing to do, but most authors don't bother. They just react whenever a change happens.

But when you're proactive, you can make the algorithms work for you.

Here's what happened with the big ebook retailers last year. Take the information in this chapter and use it to sell more books.

Amazon

No discussion of the publishing industry would be complete without Amazon. 2015 was an interesting year for the company. While there were some important news items—such as the company's forays into the textbook and children's book markets, negotiations with the Big Five, and its remodeling of the Kindle Unlimited payment program—many of the products and expanded services the company offered this year felt like quiet changes that will lay the groundwork for what the company will be doing in 2016.

If we can be sure of anything, it's that Amazon always has something in the works. For the foreseeable future, it will continue to drive the industry in new directions.

Let's get to the news.

Amazon Reveals Its Secrets about the Kindle Program

Russ Grandinetti, Kindle Senior Vice President, gave two interviews this year, giving us a glimpse into the Kindle department and its business strategies.

At a guest panel at the Digital Book World Conference and Expo in New York City, Grandinetti discussed the Amazon-Hachette dispute, agency pricing, and indie authors' concerns over Kindle Unlimited.

On the Kindle Chronicles Podcast with Len Edgerly, Grandinetti talked again about Kindle Unlimited and the recent changes to the program, Kindle Scout, and how the company looks at the marketplace and disruption.

It goes without saying that interviews with the retail giant are rare and worth paying attention to, especially when the subject is authors and self-publishing.

Takeaway: Listen to the interviews with Russ and read between the lines. His insights into how the company conceived Kindle Unlimited and the type of consumption it was intended for nails my prior speculations on the head (hint: The service was created as a way for readers to discover new authors, not to be an all-encompassing subscription service). If you understand Amazon's strategy behind Kindle Unlimited, then you understand why it's absolutely essential to think about KDP Select on a book-by-book basis instead of an all-or-nothing approach.

New Review Features

In March, Amazon added several new fields on review pages in order to help readers leave more detailed reviews.

The fields ask readers to rate things like the author's writing style, the level of violence and sexual content, point of view, and mood. These new features are similar to the spirit of the reviews on Audible.com.

It is unknown whether this new feature will help or hinder readers when leaving reviews, but it is an important thing for indie authors to pay attention to. Henry Baum at *Self-Publishing Review* broke this story, and he includes several screenshots of these new fields in his blog post. You can also view these fields in action on Amazon.com. Depending on when you read this, the feature may be in beta and there may be changes.

Takeaway: If you read your reviews, it's extra feedback.

Series Pages

Amazon has launched a series page feature that highlights all of the books in a series and allows readers to purchase them all with a single click.

There are no official reports or press releases regarding this feature or whether it will be available for all authors in the future; however, I included links to a couple of series pages in the Sources section. This feature appears to be in beta, so the look of the series pages may change slightly depending on when you view them, and it may not be available on every country's store.

Takeaway: Wait patiently. I suspect this will be available for all authors sooner than later. Successful indies might be able to email Amazon to see if they qualify for the program.

KDP EDU

Amazon continued its expansion into the academic market this year, launching its new KDP EDU program.

According to the company's press release, KDP EDU is an extension of the KDP authors platform and it is designed to "help educators and authors easily prepare, publish, and promote eTextbooks and other educational content for students to access on a broad range of devices, including Fire tablets, iPad, iPhone, Android smartphones and tablets, Mac, and PC. Educators and authors can use the new Kindle Textbook Creator tool to easily turn PDFs of their textbooks and course materials into Kindle books."

Among some of the features available to readers are multi-color highlighting, a notebook feature to capture key content, flashcards, a dictionary, and Kindle's Whispersync service so students can read their textbooks anywhere on any device.

Takeaway: If you ever had any dreams about entering the academic market, now's the time to do it. I can envision a marketplace in the next five years where progressive colleges and professors look to Amazon's textbook offerings to design their syllabi instead of relying on peer review gatekeeping. Some professors may even write their own textbooks and publish them through the service.

With device integration, and the younger generations becoming more comfortable with reading digitally, this will be a bonanza unlike anything we've seen before. I would bet money in Vegas that an indie textbook writer will write a breakout book and offer it at a fraction of what standard textbook publishers can, while still making a killing at a 70% royalty rate.

With the cost of books and tuition skyrocketing, universities are under constant pressure to provide better value for their students. Lower cost textbooks combined with technological convenience will force universities to make a change ... eventually. It will also force traditional publishers to improve their digital offerings, which right now are poor at best.

If you have an academic bent, can find the right topic that you're knowledgeable about, take on all of the responsibilities of research, content creation, top-notch editing, cover design and book formatting, and can make inroads with academic institutions, then this market is yours.

Amazon Giveaways

Amazon announced Amazon Giveaways, a feature that lets anyone facilitate a giveaway for physical products on Amazon. According to Amazon, "Everyone from authors, aspiring artists, non-profits, brands, bloggers, social media gurus and more, can now use Amazon to create a giveaway, choosing prizes from millions of eligible physical items." Amazon handles the contest entries, the shipping, and the fulfillment.

At the time of this writing, authors cannot give away ebook versions of their books, but they can do giveaways for print books.

Takeaway: It's far more expensive to use an Amazon giveaway than it is to simply order author's copies on CreateSpace. However, if you want to give away someone else's book as a prize for a contest (like on your mailing list), you could do it this way since Amazon does all the heavy lifting.

Amazon Advertising

Amazon launched Amazon Marketing Services, a pay-per-click advertising program that allows KDP Select authors to purchase targeted ads that appear on Amazon.com.

The service works similar to Facebook advertising and Google Adwords, where ads are auctioned off to the highest bidder. Authors can segment their ads based on specific genres and products. The ads appear below the buy button on product pages and on specified Kindle e-ink E-readers.

I covered Amazon Marketing Services in 2014 when it was still in beta. In general, the vibe is the same: Authors have mostly criticized the service, stating that it's not effective. Additionally, authors have complained that it could take potential sales away because the ads appear just below the buy button on product pages.

Takeaway: Unless Amazon updates the service to make it more effective, don't use it. To date, as far as I could tell, there have not been any major success stories with Amazon Marketing Services yet, which means Amazon still has some retooling to do. Facebook advertising has made a surprising comeback this year, so authors would probably be better off using the social media company's service instead.

European Union Woes

In June 2015, the European Union announced a formal investigation into Amazon's business practices in that region, citing concerns over whether certain clauses in the company's contracts with publishers constitute antitrust violations.

The EU is primarily concerned about whether these business practices affect consumers. According to EU Commissioner Margrethe Vestager: "Amazon has developed a successful business that offers consumers a comprehensive service, including for e-books. Our investigation does not call that into question. However, it is my duty to make sure that Amazon's arrangements with publishers are not harmful to consumers, by preventing other e-book distributors from innovating and competing effectively with Amazon. Our investigation will show if such concerns are justified."

Takeaway: Just stay informed. It will likely be some time before this investigation is complete. Also keep in mind that Amazon has been on the EU's radar for its Luxembourg operations (the company allegedly operates from that country due to lower tax rates). And let's not forget the VATMOSS legislation passed last year, which also affects the company.

Whether any of these antitrust allegations are true is anyone's guess. Maybe they are, maybe they aren't; but an unfavorable finding could have chilling repercussions on Amazon's business practices in the EU, the effects of which will trickle down to indie authors everywhere.

Kindle Unlimited 2.0

In June 2015, Amazon announced major changes to the Kindle Unlimited payment program, which caused a great stir in the indie author community. The company announced that it would be paying authors based on pages read instead of borrows.

How it worked before: Authors were paid every time a reader borrowed one of their books and read past the 10% mark. Payments fluctuated from between $2.00 per borrow when the program started to around $1.33 per borrow when the original payment structure ended in June. Shorter works tended to flourish because it was easier to get readers past the 10% mark.

How it works now: Amazon logs how many pages each reader reads and then uses standardized page settings in order to account for various reading differences such as font, line spacing and line height. The result is the Kindle Edition Normalized Page Count (KENPC) which, according to Amazon, "allows us to identify pages in a way that works across genres and devices." Authors are paid in proportion to how many total pages are read. The new system favors longer works because authors are paid per page. The payment per page for July 2015 was around $0.0057, which launched dozens of op-ed articles and blog posts speculating on the future of authors, payment for art, and Amazon's business practices.

Prior to the change, authors had been complaining about decreasing payouts and certain individuals who were "gaming the system" by writing short works or breaking up longer works into parts in order to maximize their chances of making money.

When Amazon announced the change, there was a fair amount of hand-wringing and anxiety from authors both inside and outside of Kindle Unlimited. Authors in the program feared even more decreased payouts. Authors outside the program worried about another "KU Apocalypse" similar to what happened in 2014 (basically, authors not enrolled in KDP Select saw their sales decrease as a result of Kindle Unlimited).

Despite the worry, little has changed. Bestselling authors such as Hugh Howey and Joe Konrath have reported increased sales, while midlist authors are generally seeing mixed results, which is exactly what happened when Kindle Unlimited launched. It's hard to know if these changes are new territory or if authors will be making the same complaints in a few months.

I covered Kindle Unlimited's inception in last year's *Indie Author State of the Union*, and I expressed the same concerns that many indie authors had about the program then. I also predicted that Amazon was going to have a crisis on its hands if it didn't do something about the Kindle Unlimited payouts. The company definitely took drastic action, but time will tell before we will know what the real impact of the new payout structure will be.

Takeaway: Decide on a book-by-book basis whether KDP Select still makes sense for your author business. Be intentional about your decision and don't imitate successful authors just because. There's nothing to say here that hasn't been discussed ad nauseum everywhere already, so do your homework if you haven't already.

Nook

I covered Barnes & Noble's Nook division extensively last year, and most of the coverage was not favorable. 2015 was still not a good year for Nook. Many are speculating that the retailer is attempting to sell Nook but has not been able to do so.

There are a lot of warning signs.

There's a new CEO who will likely shake things up.

The company recorded less than stellar profits and reportedly bought back a significant share of its stock from Microsoft.

They no longer make their own tablets (Samsung makes them).

The company closed its international stores, limiting its customer base to the United States and the United Kingdom as of August 2015.

All of these signs (and many more) indicate that change is on the horizon.

The most newsworthy item this year, however, was the company's new print on demand service, housed under its Nook Press platform. The service allows indie authors to prepare paperback and hardcover versions of their work. The service does not distribute books to Barnes & Noble.com or its retail stories, however, which makes it more similar to a vanity publisher than say, CreateSpace (which distributes books to reputable retailers).

Shortly after the POD service launched, allegations of ties to Author Solutions arose. David Gaughran wrote a well-researched article that links the two companies together by examining Nook Press's terms and conditions.

So, again—not a good media year for Nook.

Takeaway: I have a couple of suggestions:

* **Stick with CreateSpace.** If it is in fact true that Nook Press is associated with Author Solutions ... well, that's very bad news. But it's nothing the company can't fix. Plenty of reputable, large publishing industry businesses have distanced themselves from Author Solutions lately, so there's no saying Barnes & Noble won't do the same if this new venture isn't profitable.

* **Don't jump on the "let's bash Nook/Barnes & Noble" bandwagon.** I don't think Nook is going away any time soon. POD complaints aside, I actually like Nook Press's ebook service, and I want them to be able to compete against Amazon. Perhaps these new changes will allow them to do that. Competition is good, no matter how lucrative Kindle Unlimited may seem.

* **Help Nook out.** You can help ensure healthier competition by publishing your ebooks on Nook Press, linking to Nook versions of your book on your website and on your mailing list, signing up for their affiliate program, and making sure you don't discount them from your marketing strategy. This advice applies to all retailers that you do business with.

Nook may be on the decline, but they are still a powerful force in the industry, and they *can* bounce back. Too many forces are at work to be able to predict the future here.

Apple iBooks

Apple had a newsworthy year, but most of the news revolved around "cracking" the platform.

First, there was the news that iBooks was reportedly adding one million users a week after the iOS 8 launch, now that it comes pre-installed on Apple devices.

Apple also quietly accepted "assetless pre-orders" from Smashwords and Draft2Digital, allowing authors to accept payment for pre-orders of their books well ahead of publication.

Another notable news item was iBooks Author 2.3, the book publishing software that allows Mac users to create ebooks to sell on iBooks. The update comes with a number of improvements including ePub 3 support, the ability to add multimedia content, and a few other usability tweaks to enhance the reading experience on iPhones, iPads, and other ePub readers. To date, iBooks Author is only available for Mac users.

On the *Self-Publishing Podcast*, author Julia Kent offered some tips for selling more books with Apple. Dan Wood, Director of Operations and Publisher Relations at Draft2Digital, also offered some tips of his own in **a** separate interview.

In his *Your First 10K Readers* course, Nick Stephenson also uncovered some of the mystery behind Apple's iBooks store, how to optimize metadata there, and how to secure merchandising opportunities.

Takeaways: For a company that shrouds itself in relative secrecy, I find it interesting that Apple is letting almost everyone else do the talking for them. Only in one of the news items this year did they talk about their platform, and that was only to report that they were adding one million users a week to iBooks. For the *Self Publishing Podcast* interview, they declined to speak on the show (apparently they don't do interviews) and sent a successful iBooks author (Julia Kent) to speak for them instead.

Also, it bears mentioning that, at the time of this writing, it's still better to go through a distributor like Smashwords or Draft2Digital to sell books on Apple rather than selling direct. The iBooks Author update is encouraging, but until they give all authors the ability to upload directly to iBooks, it's hard to take any of their publishing tools seriously.

Yet the strange part is that Apple *is* committed to iBooks. They just aren't acting like it.

Take advantage of the promotional opportunities and read up on everything released this year. There's a lot of it. Increasing sales on Apple's platform is easier than ever, but unlike the other retailers, it takes some know-how.

Kobo

Kobo continued to build its self-publishing platform, Kobo Writing Life (KWL), this year.

The company added an Author Services section to the KWL dashboard, connecting authors with recommended partners and services to help them produce high quality books. At the time of this writing, the Author Services section is still in development, but Kobo has promised to offer recommended providers for print on demand, purchasing ISBNs, reviews with *Publishers Weekly*, pre-made book covers, cover designers, editing, and audiobooks.

Kobo also offered a 50% discount off *Publishers Weekly* for Kobo Writing Life authors in Canada and the United States for a limited time. (The offer may be expired by the time you read this).

The company has also been beta-testing a new promotions feature that will let authors apply for merchandising opportunities from within the Kobo Writing Life dashboard (I am a beta user), which is another chance for them to sell more books on the platform.

Kobo's parent company, Rakuten, also acquired OverDrive this year, fueling speculation that Kobo may be making inroads into libraries.

Takeaway: Publish your books on Kobo if you haven't already! My Kobo sales increased this year, but that was only after 18 months of being there. As I wrote in the Nook section, we need healthier competition—and it doesn't get any healthier than Kobo.

The OverDrive acquisition is very encouraging. Libraries are the next battleground for indies, and it looks like Kobo will be on the frontline, so it's imperative to have your books there. OverDrive is expanding like crazy right now, so anything is possible.

Smashwords

Smashwords had a quiet year compared to the other ebook retailers.

CEO Mark Coker spoke at Indie Recon about the most important things indie authors need to know in 2015. He also spoke to Joanna Penn on the *Creative Penn* podcast about current events in indie publishing.

In June 2015, the company announced Assetless ("Metadata Only") Pre-orders for iBooks, Barnes & Noble and Kobo, which means that authors can create pre-order pages for their books without a book file or a book cover. This new feature helps authors build momentum for their books.

In August 2015, the company announced it would be terminating its partnership with India ebook retailer Flipkart, citing irreconcilable differences with systems and technology.

Takeaway: I doubt anyone was selling any books on Flipkart anyway.

Use the pre-orders to your advantage. The rules aren't nearly as strict as Amazon's, and it's worth experimenting. Just make sure to be a good business partner and don't miss your deadlines.

And pay attention whenever Mark Coker speaks—he has his finger on the pulse of the industry. The self-publishing movement owes a great deal to him, and his thoughts on anti-exclusivity are worth adhering to.

Who Else Wants to Sell More Books on Smashwords?

Do you have trouble uploading your book to Smashwords? Does the Meat Grinder grind your ebook into meat?

Jason Matthews has created a course on Udemy called "Self-Publishing with Smashwords" that shows indie authors how to format and upload your books there for maximum effect. Newbies and pros alike will benefit from Jason's tips and tricks, and this course is the only one of its kind that focuses on optimizing your Smashwords presence.

Draft2Digital

Draft2Digital continued its expansion into the market this year, proving itself a worthy competitor to Smashwords.

The company redesigned its self-publishing dashboard to make uploading books easier.

Dan Wood, the Director of Operations and Publisher Relations, also made an appearance on the Self-Publishing Podcast to talk about ways to sell more books through the platform, particularly on Apple and Scribd. He also offered some unique insights into foreign markets.

And speaking of foreign markets, the company announced a partnership with Tolino, the German ebook retailer, allowing existing D2D authors to add their books to the platform with a single click. The company also announced a partnership with Oyster, giving authors an alternative route onto the platform (Smashwords also distributes to Oyster).

Draft2Digital also rolled out a new feature where their system will auto-generate back matter with a compelling call to action at the end. The benefit of the auto-generated back matter is that it is store-specific—so if you have Book 1 in a series and want to include links to Book 2, Draft2Digital will generate the links for you. So Apple readers will be sent to the iBooks sales page for Book 2, for example.

The company also launched a wholly-owned subsidiary company called Books2Read, which is a BookBub-like service that connects readers with indie authors. If requested, Draft2Digital will also put a signup link for Books2Read where readers can enter their email address to get updates whenever you release a new book.

Takeaway: 2015 is proof more than ever that Draft2Digital is a serious competitor in the distributor space. The Tolino and Oyster integrations were impressive. While the auto-generated back matter may not be something I use, it's an extremely powerful tool that fills a serious need. More people need to know about it, actually.

I'm positive that the company will continue its growth and will keep winning indies over. I also expect them to sign contracts with venues that indies would benefit from.

Google Play

The Google Play app has now been installed on over one billion devices.

Despite this news, authors have been hesitant to publish with Google Play because of the retailer's difficult dashboard and arbitrary price discounting. Now those authors cannot publish on the platform at all. In May 2015, Google Play announced that it would be closing its doors to new authors, citing concerns over "content management" (piracy). In an email to the *Sell More Books Show,* they pledged to fix this issue and reopen to new authors once it was fixed.

It's September 2015 as I write this article, and the Google Play store is still closed to new authors. However, existing Google Play authors are still able to use the platform without any limitations.

Takeaway: If you weren't on Google Play before the bad news dropped, you're probably kicking yourself. Despite its shortcomings, Google Play *is* a solid platform. Google Play accounts for roughly 10-15% of my income, so my experiences with the platform have been positive. I hope they open their doors to new authors soon so more people can learn how to sell books there. But something in the back of my mind tells me that there could be some bad news coming, since they've been closed this long. Google is infamous for killing its services—even popular ones. I'm not sure how committed Google is to ebooks in the long term.

Oyster and Scribd

Oyster and Scribd continued making progress in the subscription market this year. Both signed deals with Macmillan, who brought some high-profile titles to the services' catalogues.

Indie authors who publish on Draft2Digital can now publish their books on Oyster, thanks to a partnership between the two companies.

Oyster also announced an ebook store featuring titles from all of the Big Five publishers, which is available to both subscribers and non-subscribers as a way to further monetize the platform … until Oyster announced in September 2015 that it would be shutting down. It is speculated that the company was bought by an unnamed buyer, with most of the staff going to Google.

Scribd's year wasn't positive, either. In February 2015, it added more than 10,000 comic books to its subscription service.

Then, in June, the company announced that it would be removing a large number of romance and erotica titles from the platform. Many speculated that romance and erotica titles were so popular that the service couldn't sustain them.

In August, Scribd then announced that it would be dialing back its audiobook service and changing it to a credit-based system, giving subscribers one audiobook credit per month, with a new audiobook catalog that rotates every 30 days. Scribd wrote, "This change will not only allow us to continue to grow our audiobook catalog in a sustainable way, but will also allow us to focus on even more content deals and offerings we know you'll love."

Takeaways: When you compare Oyster and Scribd side by side, you can tell a lot about both companies. Oyster was much more cautious, and they grew slowly. Scribd is much more aggressive, and as a result, they have had to change their strategy in order to stay sustainable. Now that Oyster is gone, Scribd is doomed, if you ask me.

For a little while, we had some healthy competition in this space. But alas, not even an innovative company like Oyster could compete against Amazon. I'm sad to see Oyster go.

However, I still believe the best is yet to come. There are some subscription models out there that haven't even been tried yet.

I still believe that genre-based subscription services are the future. For example, romance authors could pool all of their resources into a new subscription service where romance readers pay, say $9.99 a month and get access to more romance books than they can read.

Kindle Unlimited, Oyster, and Scribd are simply vehicles of discovery; they cannot ever offer a complete catalog that will satisfy everyone. However, when you approach subscriptions by genre, it's much easier to offer a comprehensive selection of books that will satisfy even the most voracious readers of that genre. It also makes it more lucrative for traditional publishers to jump on board if the service does well. (Someone, steal this idea, please!)

Traditional Publishing

As an indie author, it's easy to overlook the developments in the traditional publishing space because, well, indies generally don't need traditional publishers.

But there were a few newsworthy events in the traditional publishing world that had a huge impact on indies.

I've always said that indie authors aren't competing against each other; they're competing against traditional publishers. And publishers have gotten smarter.

The Return of

Agency Pricing

Agency pricing is back.

Throughout 2015, Amazon continued negotiations with the rest of the Big Five publishers, signing deals that basically allowed publishers to set the prices of their books, but with incentives for them to price their books lower. However, publishers raised their prices instead. According to a September 2015 article in the *The Wall Street Journal*, ebook sales dropped.

Joe Konrath fisked the WSJ article, wondering why it took so long to figure this out. He writes, "What did Schopenhauer say? 'All truth passes through three stages. First, it is ridiculed. Second, it is violently opposed. Third, it is accepted as being self-evident.' Although if the Big Five continues to adhere to a high-priced ebook strategy, and continues to rely on insights as fresh and useful as those in this *Wall Street Journal* article, the more relevant rubric might be Elisabeth Kübler-Ross's anger, denial, bargaining, depression, acceptance."

The September Author Earnings Report also shows a decline in ebook sales as a result of agency pricing (covered later in this book).

Takeaway: It's still too soon to say whether the higher ebook prices are truly responsible for the drop in publishers' revenue, or if it can be explained by something else. Sometimes sales drop, and then rise higher than they were before. That very well could happen, just as much as sales could continue to drop. I'll bet on the latter, but it's too soon to tell. Expect this to be a hot news item in 2016.

On another note, I would like to point out a trend that I noticed but don't have any data to support: Traditional publishers are adopting indie promotion techniques to make those higher prices more palatable.

I have been seeing price promotions from traditional publishers that weren't being done previously. For example, I encountered several traditionally published books that were priced at $0.99-$2.99 for a price promotion, possibly as a result of a promotional ad like BookBub. I am also seeing more traditionally published books using the first book in a series as a loss leader. I know this because I purchased several cheap first books in a series. I even found some free ones by traditional publishers.

Publishers are also getting savvier with mailing lists and calls to actions in the backs of their books, taking after successful indies. Earlier this year, I joined a Simon & Schuster mailing list that offered a slew of $0.99 books just for signing up. This was unheard of just a year ago.

If you aren't taking advantage of price promotions, CTAs, and mailing lists, you're already behind the curve. Way behind.

In lieu of traditional publishing's advancements, it's going to get harder for indies to sell books, so this should be a wake-up call. Being an author is fun, but at the end of the day, this is a business, and the big boys are playing tougher. If you're going to succeed in 2016, you'll have to roll up your sleeves.

Author Solutions
and Friends

David Gaughran wrote a revealing blog post with an update about the lawsuit against Author Solutions. He connects several reputable publishing companies with the service, attacking them for using Author Solutions to power their publishing services.

Among the companies mentioned in the post are Publishers Weekly, Kirkus, Barnes & Noble, Penguin Random House, Harlequin, Simon & Schuster, and Writer's Digest. Since Gaughran's article, several of the companies listed have terminated their partnership with Author Solutions.

Gaughran also discusses the company's business practices and how it puts pressure on its sales representatives to meet quotas.

Takeaway: I kept this article brief because David Gaughran's journalism and eloquence covers this topic better than I ever could. My heart hurts for all the authors who have been embroiled in this fiasco. Sadly, the lawsuit was dismissed.

But there's an important lesson here.

Learning how to be an author is not difficult. The information is out there; all you have to do is look for it. If some of the authors involved with Author Solutions had done their homework, they would have discovered that they didn't need Author Solutions in the first place.

When you don't have the right information, you can't make good business decisions, which is the reason I created the *Indie Author State of the Union* series. Too many authors have absolutely no understanding of what it means to be an author and businessperson. There will always be authors who fall prey to deceptive publishing practices, but *you* can take some simple steps today to make sure that you don't become one of those casualties.

First, stop looking for shortcuts. Authors with the "shortcut mentality" always get ripped off.

Second, be willing to do the work. Recognize that it's going to take time, blood, sweat, and tears to be a successful author. Few successful authors got where they are without paying the price for that success. That price, unfortunately, means making some sacrifices that you may not be comfortable with. But it doesn't mean paying exorbitant sums of money for a publishing package.

Third, always make sure you read the terms of service and the privacy policy for any service, application, or platform that you use. Seriously, read them. *If you don't agree with something in the conditions, don't use the service!* Otherwise, you'll wake up one day with a legal headache, and you'll have only yourself to blame.

And finally, for heaven's sake, hire an intellectual property attorney to advise you before signing *any* kind of publishing agreement. IP attorneys aren't cheap, but neither is having to rebuild your career because you didn't understand a contract. In my humble opinion, a lawyer's opinion before entering into a contract is dirt cheap compared the latter. Dirt cheap, indeed.

The Real Price of Traditional Publishing

Dean Wesley Smith shared his thoughts on traditional publishing in the year 2015 in a blog post titled "The Real Price of Traditional Publishing."

Smith, a prolific author who started on the traditional route but who is now pro-indie, talks about why he believes traditional publishing is a bad idea for authors in this new publishing landscape. He cites falling advances and bad contract terms as the major changes that are hurting traditionally published authors, and he also has some choice words for literary agents.

Takeaway: I am a big fan of Dean Wesley Smith and believe that more authors should be paying attention to his advice (the same goes for his wife, Kristine Kathryn Rusch). Dean has been in the industry for a long time and knows its ins and outs; new and young authors can learn a lot from him and apply his advice to their careers.

Libraries

2015 was the year of the library—at least in the United States.

In an article titled "Cautions on E-Books," librarian Daniel Goldstein lays out the problems librarians face with ebooks and digital reading. He suggests that libraries are often limited in what they can do with their ebook acquisitions because their ebooks are licensed. According to Goldstein, under the first sale doctrine in the United States, libraries historically have been able to do whatever they want with their books because they own the books. Because ebooks are *licensed* from third-party vendors like 3M and OverDrive, libraries do not have the same rights. As a result, acquisitions and interlibrary loans are expensive.

According to the Douglas County Libraries in Colorado, who releases pricing comparisons between libraries and consumers each year, libraries have to pay approximately $19-$90 per copy of an average bestseller ebook license, when consumers only pay $2.99-$11.99 per book. According to Joe Konrath, ebook vendors also require libraries to renew their ebook licenses, so libraries have to keep paying for the same acquisitions. This is different compared to print books, which are paid for once and then completely owned (as discussed in Goldstein's article).

A few companies emerged this year with aspirations to help libraries solve this problem. The first is Ebooks Are Forever, created by Joe Konrath and August Wainwright, which aims to help librarians and indie authors by providing them high quality, low cost acquisitions. Per the company website, their goal is "[to] offer a large, curated collection of ebooks to every library in North America, at a fair and *sustainable* price, where the library owns the ebook forever and authors and publishers make great, ongoing royalties."

At the time of this writing, Ebooks Are Forever charges libraries approximately $7.99 for novels and $3.99-$4.99 for shorter works. They pay 70% royalties to the author. Libraries own the ebook forever and can use it however they wish. Accordingly, if patrons ask librarians for a certain title, they can pass the word to Ebooks Are Forever, who will then do the legwork to acquire the title.

Ebooks Are Forever is still in beta and is invitation-only at the time of this writing, but authors are still encouraged to apply to see if their books will be accepted.

Another avenue into libraries is Self-e, a partnership between *Library Journal* and *Biblioboard*. The service provides vetted, curated books to state and national libraries in the United States, and is open to authors around the world as long as their books are in English. According to Porter Anderson, who wrote an in-depth article about the program, authors can apply to get their books selected for the program, but do not receive any royalties despite the fact that libraries do pay to acquire the books. In essence, the service is purely a vehicle for discovery, which is something that participating authors will need to be comfortable with (Anderson directs readers to an article on the Self-e site called "Is Self-e Right for Me?" to help with the decision). Anderson also provides a cursory review of some of the program's terms and services.

Takeaway: I made a lot of predictions last year, but I had no idea that libraries would be in the news so much in 2015. It felt like there was a new story about libraries every week.

I believe we may be at a tipping point, where the distribution method for libraries will change. It's going to get easier to "crack" libraries.

Ebooks Are Forever is really exciting. If Konrath succeeds, the game changes.

Self-e is also interesting. While I am not crazy about the lack of payment, there are numerous benefits to being in a library. As always, do your homework and read the terms of service. Make the best decision for your business. Porter Anderson's article is a must-read before making your decision.

This isn't the end for libraries. Expect to keep seeing them in the news.

International Markets

Foreign markets are still burgeoning, and it's important to know what's going on around the world. Global events *will* impact your author business.

Just about every emerging market had some great news this year, but I couldn't include every one. There's far more happening in the world than what you'll read here.

If you want to learn in-depth information about a particular market, I recommend that you check out the Global Ebook Report—it's an extremely well-researched yearly report of what's happening in every country around the world. It's a bit expensive but very insightful. You can also perform a Google search for something like "China ebook market 2015" and you'll get more stories than you can read. That's how explosive ebooks are around the world.

Here's the global news.

Mexico & Latin America

Amazon announced its Second Annual Indie Literary Prize for self-published authors in Spanish-speaking countries. The contest allows Spanish-language authors to submit previously unpublished manuscripts for the chance to win a publishing deal with Amazon to get their book into English, print and audio formats.

In other Spanish-language news, Kobo announced a groundbreaking partnership with two of Mexico's largest book retailers, Libreria Porrúa and Gandhi, in order to bring 70,000 ebooks to Mexican readers via a new service called Orbile, which allows readers to access curated bestsellers, literary works, comics, graphic novels, and children's books. Per Kobo's press release, this content will be available on any device, and the new service will go live in September 2015.

Mexico has proven itself to be the biggest Spanish-language market for ebook growth (it's the second largest book economy in Central and South America after Brazil). In a report titled "The Bookwire Spanish and Portuguese Digital Markets Report," several Mexican industry professionals paint an extremely detailed, number-focused picture of the Mexican book market. Among some of the key takeaways: Traditional publishing houses still have the most control in the region, 57% of new titles in 2014 were produced by national institutions, and brick-and-mortar retailers are still the key sales channels (as evidenced by Kobo's partnership above). The report concludes that "The stagnation of the traditional book market, on-going development of e-commerce structures and publishers' expanding range of digital products could lead to a real explosion of digital commerce in the region within the next decade."

These developments could prepare Mexico to be one of the next big battlegrounds in the publishing world.

Takeaway: As far as burgeoning markets go, I'd put money on Mexico and all of Latin America (and Brazil). Spanish is one of the most common languages in the world, and the Mexican publishing economy seems ripe for explosive growth.

I wouldn't extend that same enthusiasm to Spain, however, for reasons in the next article.

European Union

Meanwhile, across the Atlantic, the European Union struggled with ebooks.

The European Union passed its controversial VATMOSS (Value-Added Tax Mini One-Stop Shopping) tax laws, which levy taxes on digital services based on where customers are located (compared to where the business is located). This has indirectly affected ebooks and indie authors, since ebooks and digital courses are considered services under the EU laws, and ebook prices are now VAT-inclusive. Authors must either price their books higher to make up for the VAT hike, or keep their prices the same and accept lower margins.

This is a high-level overview of the complex laws—there have been plenty of articles written on the topic. If you still can't wrap your head around the laws, see the Sources section for a helpful flowchart.

Takeaway: The VATMOSS law was disappointing, but I think the EU will bounce back and reform it. There's already talk of the law being reformed.

However, this brings up a bitter topic that indies will have to face soon: All ebooks and audiobooks are going to be taxed. I don't think it's unreasonable to predict that many countries will start following the EU's lead in the next decade, especially if the ebook market share continues to grow. And honestly, given the tremendous growth, can you blame governments for wanting to tax ebooks?

In the United States at least, Amazon has been doing its best to stave off taxes on its physical goods, but it appears to be slowly losing that battle. I think we're all going to have to get comfortable with the idea that taxes on ebooks are probably here to stay.

France

France struggled with ebooks this year.

An EU court sued France and Luxembourg for not levying enough taxes on ebooks, ruling that ebooks were considered services, not goods. The court opined that a reduced tax rate could only apply to goods (read: physical books). This ruling may set the stage for further taxation issues for ebooks in the EU.

That's not all for French news. The French Minister of Culture, Fleur Pellerin, took issue with Kindle Unlimited because she alleged that it violated the country's Lang Law, which requires that publishers control the price of an ebook (read: price-fixing). Because Amazon controls the payouts of the books in Kindle Unlimited, French officials believed the service was illegal. The French courts agreed (though they believed that ebook subscription services in and of themselves *were* legal). It is unknown exactly what steps Amazon will have to take to modify their French business strategy. It is also important to note that this ruling affected several other ebook subscription companies in France—they too were forced to bring their services into compliance with French laws.

Takeaway: When you hear people say France isn't friendly toward ebooks or indie authors, this is why. Honestly, it goes even deeper than what I covered here. The French's approach to ebooks is backwards at best, but they'll come around. That being said, unless you're a bestseller with tremendous print presence, I wouldn't translate your books into French.

Germany

German ebook retailer Tolino launched its self-publishing platform this year, giving German authors the ability to indie publish their books. English-speaking indies can also distribute their books on the platform through Smashwords or Draft2Digital.

In terms of growth, it appears that the ebook market in Germany has stabilized somewhat. The German Publishers and Booksellers Association estimates the ebook marketshare at 4.3%. According to Edward Nawotka at Publishing Perspectives, "The general consensus is that Amazon has an ebook marketshare of 50-60%, Tolino 15-20%, and Apple 10%." In the article, Nawotka cites concerns over Tolino's ability to compete as a brick-and-mortar store and e-reader manufacturer in a changing German economy where mobile phone reading is increasing. He also suggests that ebook subscription services such as Kindle Unlimited could further erode Tolino's future ability to compete.

Takeaway: The German market may have stabilized, but this isn't the end. Tolino has shown itself to be a worthy competitor to Amazon, so I'm positive that they'll adapt. In many ways, they're like a young Barnes & Noble (Tolino is actually a consortium of German bookstores and publishers, including Bertelsmann, who owns Penguin Random House). They have a brick-and-mortar presence, a lot of connections, and an e-reader division—just like Barnes & Noble. I just hope that Tolino is taking notes from the American book giant's misfortunes.

In my opinion, Germany is still a safe bet for indie authors in the long run. If I had a few spare thousand dollars laying around, I'd probably spend them on a German translation.

China

China is the second largest ebook market in the world.

The Chinese love their mobile devices, and smartphone and tablet reading are dominant there. A national survey came out this year stating that ebooks have now become the primary reading medium in China, with 58.4% of adults surveyed reading digitally.

I imagine that a statistician might quibble with the statistics in any Chinese survey, given the number of people surveyed vs. the number of people in China. However, Vearsa, a distributor for publishers, visited the country in an effort to further understand the Chinese ebook market. In an insightful two-part blog post, Digital Marketing Manager Patrick Crowley writes, "What became clear to us very quickly is that the market in China is quite fragmented. There are a number of industries in the hunt for eBook revenues: online retailers, hardware manufacturers, social networks, telecom operators, search engines and even traditional brick-and-mortar stores. Gareth [Vearsa CEO] and I met with a number of the key players in these industries and it appears that as of today, while the choices for Chinese language eBooks are widespread, there really are only a limited number of options for selling non-Chinese language content into China."

According to the 2014 Global Ebook Report by Rüdiger Wischenbart, there are other unique problems in the Chinese ebook market: One distributor controls most of the market, and all of the publishing houses there are owned by the state, which means that authors and publishers have to deal with censorship and altering of their content. Not to mention piracy concerns.

This article doesn't even begin to scratch the surface of how complex the Chinese market is. As the industry moves forward, expect it to be a major player unlike any we've ever seen.

Takeaway: I'll be honest—researching sources for the *Indie Author State of the Union* series is fun. I enjoy it tremendously. But trying to wrap my head around China gave me constant anxiety. It still does. When I say that this market is difficult to comprehend, I mean that in every sense of the word. As an indie author, the untapped potential excites me, but the country's censorship would keep me up at night if I ever pursued a publishing contract there.

Which brings me to another point. It's easy to assume that what happened in the United States, Canada, United Kingdom and Australia will also happen in the rest of the world. If you take most of the publishing news articles that you read at face value, it's an easy assumption.

But the truth is, every country's publishing economy is different in ways that we can't understand from the comfort of our couches, myself included. The history of ebooks in each country will not be the same.

The reason the ebook movement is so revolutionary is not because of ebooks themselves, but because of the daring innovation of indie authors who took their lives into their own hands and made a living from their art. I personally believe that authors in every country can benefit from going indie—but only if they have the tools, knowledge and boldness to take the leap. And only if the culture and economy changes to favor them.

During my "State of the Union" travels, I encountered a huge number of organizations that provide digital publishing services for global traditional publishing houses, but I saw very few that offered these same services to global authors and aspiring authors. As the international markets mature, I see a business and an altruistic need here. For example, a group of bestselling authors could create a non-profit partnership with a self-publishing platform in Mexico that assesses the market and gives Mexican indie authors the tools they need to succeed not just in the Mexican market, but abroad.

Right now, U.S. authors are focusing on getting their books into international markets, but in the next decade, authors from emerging markets will start trying to get their books into *our* markets, and I don't think anyone is prepared for that. There is going to be a dire need for translators who can translate into English. I also see the rise of a new kind of professional—a hybrid between a translator, publicist, and literary agent who translates a book but also provides English market guidance and promotional assistance for foreign authors. It's an intriguing business idea, but also presents some opportunity for scam artists.

Ironically, this kind of hybrid professional is exactly what English-language authors need right now when they translate their books into foreign markets. They're out there, but they're usually expensive. As the international markets mature, savvy bilingual professionals can make a place for themselves by helping emerging authors.

Business

I can't stress enough the importance of being a shrewd businessperson. Fortunately, there were many, many resources released this year to help authors do this. In fact, there were so many that I couldn't include them all.

Here are some of the most useful tools that will help you take your business to the next level.

The Secret to Pricing

Your Book

With agency pricing's return and book prices fluctuating, it's always necessary for indie authors to evaluate their pricing. Two great articles provided some help with that decision.

Wise Ink published an article called "The Definitive Guide to Pricing Your Book" that explores pricing and several theories that Internet marketers use when pricing their books. While some authors may be familiar with these theories, the article is a detailed refresher, with many links to other sources so authors can do more research if they desire.

Kiss Metrics also published an article called "8 Psychological Triggers to Optimize Your Pricing Page" that explores pricing in even greater detail. It uses case studies to show different pricing theories in action.

Both articles are actionable, and authors can start to use the knowledge as soon as possible.

Takeaway: I love these articles. The *Wise Ink* article is worth glancing over, and the *Kiss Metrics* blog post is a firehose of information (like all *Kiss Metrics* blog posts are). I'm a big believer in learning from successful Internet marketers. It seems like everything they do, authors eventually start doing three to five years later, anyway.

Here is a Method to Eliminate the Risk of Carpal Tunnel Syndrome

Authors often overlook the potential for repetitive stress injuries (RSIs) like carpal tunnel syndrome, but in this case, ignorance is not bliss.

In a guest post at *The Creative Penn*, author Marianne Sciucco shares how she dealt with a devastating RSI injury, and how it put a halt on her writing career. She identifies the key symptoms of repetitive stress injuries, when to get help, and how to modify your workstation to protect yourself.

Takeaway: This article scared me when I read it for the first time. I do my best to avoid RSIs however I can, but I never imagined that they could stop your career like they almost did for Sciucco.

Repetitive stress injuries are real, and they're not fun. Read the article and start making changes. I adopted dictation this year. I am also making an effort to take short breaks every hour when I write.

Often, making the simplest lifestyle changes and committing to them yields the greatest results.

This is How a Book Becomes a Movie

Jane Friedman wrote a blog post detailing the process of how a book becomes a movie. She outlines what she believes are the four stages of the process: the pitch, the option, development, and production.

The article is insightful and informative for anyone who is not familiar with the movie-making process.

Friedman also wrote a post on how to sell your screenplay.

Takeaway: I don't know about you, but Hollywood is mysterious to me. It's good to get this kind of perspective, even if the chances of your book becoming a smash Hollywood hit are low. I believe that authors should at least know their potential options.

These Self-Publishing Videos Will Blow Your Mind

During the 2015 London Book Fair, The Alliance of Independent Authors hosted a digital event called Indie Recon 2015, where a staggering number of successful indie authors and publishing professionals hosted webinars on topics relevant to nearly every aspect of the publishing industry.

The videos are hosted on YouTube and available for anyone to watch. For free.

The events list needs to be seen to be believed, but here were some of the highlights:

* What Indie Authors Need to Know Now with Mark Coker and Orna Ross
* 10 Million Sold and Counting: Barbara Freethy and Bella Andre
* Content Marketing 101 with Jane Friedman
* How to Protect Your Rights and Your Wallet with Helen Sedwick
* How to Make a Living with Your Writing by Joanna Penn
* Book Design Basics by Joel Friedlander
* Self-Publishing in India by Rasana Atreya
* How to Optimize Your Ad for BookBub

This list is just a fraction of the content available on Indie Recon. The topics are also sorted by level (beginner, intermediate, advanced) so authors can watch them at their own pace.

Takeaway: This is hands-down the best author event in the history of self-publishing. It's an extravaganza! There are so many of them it's ridiculous. Stop what you are doing and go check out the website—you'll be blown away, I guarantee.

Author Earnings: What You Need to Know

Hugh Howey and Data Guy released a well-received Author Earnings Reports this year, chronicling the rapid changes in the publishing industry.

In the January Author Earnings Report, they pointed out that 30% of self-published books did not have ISBNs, 33% of the books on Amazon were indie-published, and indie authors took home 40% of all the revenue generated on Amazon. In essence, the report concluded that ISBNs were not necessary for indie authors, did not provide any monetary benefits, and that the industry reports by Bowker in Nielsen are wrong. They write, "What we can say for sure is that the clear lack of any material benefit in the marketplace makes the cost of purchasing an ISBN for an ebook very difficult to justify—the same money would be far better invested instead in better professional editing, proofreading, formatting, cover art, and the like."

In the May Author Earnings Report, Howey and Data Guy explored the effect of agency pricing's return on the industry in light of the Big Five's negotiations with Amazon. They concluded that traditionally published book prices rose, while publishers' profits declined. In a prophetic closing statement, they wrote, "Through all of this, we can see that control over pricing is enormously powerful. The largest retailers and the largest publishers are willing to do great harm to one another in a fight for this power. For authors who want control over their pricing so they can avoid becoming casualties in wars between retailers and publishers, the choice of publication method is clear. And it's becoming more clear every quarter, as self-published authors continue to win market share, and continue to take control of their careers."

In the September Author Earnings Report, Howey and Data Guy challenged the idea that the ebook market was shrinking. In perhaps their most popular report yet, they concluded that it was, in fact, the publisher's ebook market share that was shrinking, not the market overall. They write, "Today, traditionally-published authors are barely earning 40% of all Kindle ebook royalties paid, while self-published indie authors and those published by Amazon's imprints are taking home almost 60%. From an author-earnings perspective, in 18 short months, the U.S. ebook market has flipped upside down."

In the October Earnings Report, Howey and Data Guy explored the rest of the ebook market and discovered that Amazon makes up 74% of the market and Apple, Barnes & Noble, Kobo and Google Play control the remaining 26%. On the non-Amazon retailers, indie authors accounted for 22% of all ebooks sold. The big takeaway from the report is that the ebook market is at least 50% bigger than Nielsen and Bowker says it is.

Takeaway: I love the Author Earnings Report. When the first report came out last year, I remember how traditional publishing spewed vitriol, claiming that it was inaccurate. Almost everyone who was anyone in the traditional publishing world had an opinion about it. Basically, they HATED it. And yes, I'm using the word "hate," but even that's an understatement.

As of September 2015, there is hardly any vitriol at all. In fact, very few outlets covered the groundbreaking September report, and there were little to no "response" articles that tried to refute it.

Funny how things change. I think the traditional publishing world is finally paying attention.

Data doesn't lie.

If Howey and Data Guy are correct, 2015 just became a watershed year. This is a really big deal, because indie authors now control the majority of the ebook marketplace. I expect that next year we'll see publishers take drastic moves to recapture their marketshare, and competition is going to get even fiercer than it is today. This is good—maybe then someone will figure out the answer to discoverability.

Get Rid of Tax Headaches Once and For All with This Book

Did you know that you have to pay taxes on your book earnings?

Does your head hurt already?

It doesn't have to be this way. At least, not for U.S authors. Tax professional E. M. Lynley wrote a book called *The 2015 Author's Tax Workshop* that explains everything you need to know about taxes, tax laws, and how to set up your bookkeeping. The book is easy to read, makes taxes simple, and it will save you hours of frustration at tax time.

I used the techniques in this book to improve my bookkeeping, and when I saw my refund I went into the parking lot and did cartwheels.

OK, so I didn't *actually* do cartwheels, but boy did I want to!

Every author's tax situation is different, and their mileage will vary when using Lynley's book. It is *not* a substitute for talking to a licensed tax professional, but it will help you articulate yourself to one.

Here's How to Change Your Attitude Before It Destroys Your Career

In 2015, Kristine Kathryn Rusch blogged weekly on her *Business Rusch* blog, offering opinions on news items in the publishing industry. She collected a handful of her blog posts into a new book called *The Write Attitude*, designed to help authors avoid self-limiting mindsets by offering her trademark blunt advice backed up by her many decades of experience as a successful author.

Rusch tackles habits and routines and why authors need them, chasing trends, "getting by" as an author without doing what it really takes to be successful, and following the crowd, among other things.

Rusch is often maligned by indie authors for her opinions, but here's what I believe: You're either at the point in your career where her advice works for you, or you're not ready for it yet. But Rusch knows her stuff, and the savvy authors and business owners are paying attention to her.

Little-Known Ways to Make Short Stories Pay Big Bucks

Plenty of books teach how to write short stories, but few teach how to make money from them. And when I say make money, I mean serious money. A sustainable income.

Douglas Smith wrote a groundbreaking book called *Playing the Short Game* that gives authors a step-by-step method for monetizing short fiction in order to win readers and improve the sales of their books.

Smith's book is a business book with shrewd advice. He advocates writing the best stories you can, submitting your stories to paying markets (not free markets), avoiding simultaneous submissions, and keeping your stories on the market until they are sold.

Smith also gives advice on working with editors and negotiating magazine contracts.

Takeaway: *Playing the Short Game* is hands down the best book on the business of short stories that I have ever read. I applied Smith's techniques to a poetry collection I wrote this year, and my poems started getting published in professional magazines within two months.

If short story submissions are part of your business model, you need to read this book. If you write enough good stories, they can be great supplemental income. You might even be able to make a living from them.

Build a Career You Can Be Proud Of With This Book

How many times have you heard this statement?

"So much in life revolves around your mindset."

But when Honorée Corder says it, you believe it.

Corder released a book called *Prosperity for Writers* which aims to help indie authors overcome self-limiting beliefs. Corder is a savvy entrepreneur, business coach, and professional ass-kicker with twenty-five years of experience, so she understands the mental roadblocks that even the most successful people have, and how to break those blocks down.

Her main message is this: The myth of the starving artist is garbage.

All of us have limiting beliefs, whether we like to admit it or not. *Prosperity for Writers* will help you take stock of yourself. It's a refreshing dose of raw honesty mixed with actionable tips that you can follow immediately to change your mindset and grow your author business.

How to Write an Author Business Plan That Doesn't Suck

Have you ever tried to put together an author business plan?

If you're anything like me, you've searched all over, but none of the templates for other businesses work well for authors. They are too generic and most of the sections don't apply to what we do.

Ryan Petty, an experienced business owner, consultant and self-published author, published his book *CreateSpace & Kindle Author Business Plans Made Easy: How Indie Authors Can Think Ahead to Sell More Books, Accelerate Growth & Sustain Self-Publishing Success* (formerly titled *The Write Livelihood*), in which he details exactly how authors should think about writing their business plans.

Petty, a former nonprofit CEO whose background is in economic development, understands business plans. His ideas are worth exploring.

I've been saying for the last two years that there are plenty of "business" books on the market, but still very few that teach authors how to actually be businesspeople. There's a serious need for seasoned business people who can distill basic business principles and filter them through the lens of an author. Petty does that and much more.

The Killer Book That Will Blow Up the Poetry World

I'm allowed at least one shameless plug per year, aren't I?

I predicted last year that literary fiction and poetry would at last enter the digital world. And I was right—it's happening.

With the return of agency pricing, this just might be the watershed moment that will push poets over the edge.

I also write poetry, and I couldn't figure out for the life of me why more poets haven't self-published their work. So I wrote a book called *Indie Poet Rock Star: The Poet's Guide to Ebooks, Marketing and the Self-Publishing Revolution*. I wrote it to see if I could figure out how to sell more copies of my poetry. But it evolved into much more. Indie Poet Rock Star is my vision for what the poetry world can and should look like. I offer some interesting ways for poets to monetize their work, and I also explore some interesting partnerships they can make with indie fiction authors (which is why I included it in this year's SOTU).

Keep your fingers crossed for me, and pass the word on to any starving poets you know.

Copyright &

Intellectual Property

Indie authors don't often deal with the law, but when they do, it's usually not good.

Here's a legal update on a few things you need to know.

The Gravity of
Getting Screwed

Bestselling author Tess Gerritsen sued Warner Bros., alleging that they made the movie *Gravity* (based on the book of the same name that she authored) without properly compensating her for it.

Gerritsen sold the film rights to the book to New Line Productions in 1999. The film was slated for production, but then Warner Bros. acquired New Line in 2008, in what was apparently an unfriendly takeover. Shortly after that, an "original screenplay" for the movie *Gravity* as we know it appeared without any credit to Gerritsen, and Warner Bros. produced the movie without compensating Gerritsen per the terms of her contract with New Line.

The courts dismissed Gerritsen's **case** and upheld Warner Bros.' contention that while it did have the rights to *Gravity,* it did not have to honor the contract between Gerritsen and New Line. Gerritsen appealed, and lost again. She writes, "The court ruled that Warner Bros. is not liable for New Line's contractual obligations to me. Nor can I sue for copyright infringement, as my *Gravity* film rights are owned by New Line. The only entity with the legal standing to sue for copyright infringement is New Line—and they will certainly not sue their parent company, Warner Bros. This ruling allows me no possibility of remedy. Even if the Warner Bros.'s film had copied my story word for word, there would be nothing I could do about it."

Takeaway: If this doesn't scare you, it should, because it sets a precedent that screws authors. While I am not familiar with the exact details of Gerritsen's case, it stands to reason that a contract is a contract and should be upheld, even in an acquisition.

When authors think about signing publishing contracts, they don't often think about what would happen if that publishing company gets acquired by competitor. However, there *are* clauses you can insert in a contract to account for this type of event; they basically state that the publisher/studio/etc. cannot assign their rights or ownership to another party without the author's written consent.

Gerritsen is an extremely smart author, and I'm willing to bet that she covered all of her bases when she did the film deal. I'm sure her contract had all the necessary clauses to protect her—and she *still* got screwed. Her story should reinforce the fact that you need an intellectual property attorney to look over all of your contracts. Even if your contracts are bulletproof, there is always the chance that the other party won't do the right thing.

I don't envy Gerritsen, and I would hate to be embroiled in an intellectual property lawsuit like this one. I'm sure you don't like the idea of litigation, either, so be careful out there.

Attorney Reviews His Own Self-Published Book for Legal Issues

Attorney and self-published author Marc Whipple reviewed his own book, *My Mother Had Me Tested!* for legal issues in order to show authors legal issues that can arise out of authorship.

Whipple reviewed the font and image licensing for his cover design, his book title for potential trademark infringement, and certain references to real people both named and unnamed for potential defamation, among other things.

Takeaway: This article is notable because it highlights common issues that indie authors face but don't think (enough) about. You should also read the handful of articles on Whipple's site—he does a great job of breaking down the law in laymen's terms.

Also, if you haven't read the *Copyright Handbook*, it's a good idea to do so. It will help you avoid the many of the issues that Whipple writes about, too.

This is What Happens When Authors Die

Who owns your digital afterlife?

That's the title of an article by Matt O'Brien at Mercury News, in which he writes about the estate battle of the author Marsha Mehran, a literary bestseller who died unexpectedly. Her family could not access her email, social media and other accounts because they didn't have her passwords.

The article explores the current debate going on in California between companies like Google, AOL, Facebook and Yahoo and the families of deceased who are trying to obtain their loved ones' private information. Currently, privacy laws favor the deceased and the corporations who hold their accounts—a dead person's data remains private even after death. Even though the data exists, it is lost forever, no different than it being erased.

Mehran's family succeeded in obtaining some of her data, but not all of it, which should be a caution tale for all authors.

Joanna Penn also conducted an insightful interview with attorney Kathryn Goldman that discusses what authors need to do to protect their literary heritage.

Takeaway: I don't know about you, but the idea of what will happen to my books after I die worries me. Sure, my wife and daughter will inherit the copyrights, but they aren't as authorpreneurial as I am. Hard to think that if I got hit by a bus tomorrow, my books might slowly disappear over time.

However, it doesn't have to be this way. This isn't legal advice by any means, but here are some steps I took earlier this year to protect my digital afterlife:

1. **I learned copyright.** I studied the lives of famous authors and how they handled their estates. I also read Kristine Kathryn Rusch's blog series on estate planning. I also reread the Copyright Handbook by Stephen Fishman for the 3rd time.

2. **I established a formal system for backing up my work.** I back up all of my work religiously in multiple formats. On my computer. On an external hard drive. On a jump drive. I then separate those mediums: I keep a hard drive at home, another with a relative who doesn't live with me, and one in a secure bank deposit box. I swap them regularly so they're all up to date. The last thing I want is my work dying along with me.

3. **I met with a licensed attorney and drafted a will.** We went over my options, and I specified my literary executor and the beneficiaries of my copyrights.

4. **I created a separate document for my executor that outlines my last wishes.** In my personal experience, my will only outlines who gets what. It doesn't go into detail about "how" my estate needs to be handled. My attorney only focused on the legal aspect of it all. So in this separate document, I outlined the long-term plans for my business, my vision for the future, where my books are uploaded (and passwords), how to price my books, how to market them, etc. I stored this document along with my will.

5. **I discussed my plans with my family.** Everyone's on the same page about what will happen if I were to pass prematurely.

Those are some of the few steps I took. I'm not finished yet. But it's a good start.

You can do the same things, and you should also review your options with your attorney.

None of us are promised tomorrow. Take a few hours today and secure your legacy. When you're sipping margaritas in the afterlife, you'll be glad you did.

Cover Design and Formatting

Some great, cost-effective resources for better book cover design and formatting came out this year.

If either of these are a pain point for your author business, keep reading.

A Tale of 50 Covers Mashed Together

Programmer Jason Van Gumster designed a script that compiled the top 50 book covers from the top genres on Amazon and mashed them all together into a single, jumbled-up image.

While this sounds a little strange, Van Gumster discovered some very interesting trends among genres, such as finding commonalties in color palettes, title and author font sizes, and composition.

For example, he writes, "science fiction and fantasy show a more triangular composition while Westerns, Horror, and Romance have a more circular focal point." (He uses an image to illustrate this).

Van Gumster will be using his script to make other observations about book covers on the Kindle Store in the future.

Takeaway: I highly recommend you read this article. Van Gumster's advice sounds very generic at first, but there are a lot of layers to it. This is a powerful article if you truly want to understand the art and science of cover design. I've seen people say "X genre has this or that on the cover," but I've never seen anyone provide any actual hard data to back up those claims.

It's important to know what should go on the cover of your book. It's also important to know how your book will fit into the genre. But it's absolutely essential to know what kind of effect your book will have on readers when they see it for the first time. When you can engineer an emotional response, you can get readers to take action and buy your book. This article will help you do that.

Two New Fonts That Will Change the Way We Read

In summer 2015, Amazon announced a new font for its Kindle devices called Bookerly, which aims to solve some of the problems with the Kindle reading experience.

Bookerly is an elegant serif font that was built from scratch specifically for the Kindle ecosystem, designed for screen reading. According to John Brownlee in an article on *FastCompany*, the font is part of an "all-new layout engine that introduces better text justification, kerning, drop caps, image positioning, and more." Brownlee's article goes in-depth into the font, with many screenshots that show why it's a better font than Caecilia (Kindle's previous default font).

Google also unveiled a new font called Literata for its Google Books, also designed for screen reading. According to Nate Swanner at *The Next Web*, the font draws inspiration from Scotch and Roman fonts, and is Google's attempt to distinguish its reading experience from Nook and Kindle.

Takeaway: New fonts are a good thing, especially as screen reading increases. On the Kindle, Baskerville is still my favorite font, but compared to Bookerly, it does look less refined.

History lesson: As society progresses, fonts do, too. Look it up sometime. The history of fonts is fascinating—*Thinking with Type* by Ellen Lupton is a great read. Probably one of the most interesting books I've read in a long time. Fonts and typefaces have a long, storied history that will surprise you. When you look at their history compared to how ebook retailers are using them today, it's funny how some things never change.

What All Authors Should Know About Book Formatting

Did you know that the best tool for formatting your ebooks is 100% free?

That tool is Calibre.

Jason Matthews released a course on Udemy this year that helps indie authors take full advantage of the program to create the most professional ebooks on the market.

In this course, you'll discover how to make edits to your book without having to recompile it, how to fix table of content errors, how to optimize your metadata so that your book will be discovered easier, and much more.

I took the course earlier this year and was blown away by all the things Calibre can do. I had no idea.

And that's not all!

Jason also released a course on paperback formatting for CreateSpace with Microsoft Word.

If paperback formatting gives you the shakes, this is your course. Matthews covers the parts of a paperback and why you need to know them, how to format your margins, how to insert images in your book, and how to solve common CreateSpace errors.

Previously, if you wanted to learn paperback formatting, you had to wade through CreateSpace forums or find blog posts that only briefly cover the topic. Few in-depth video courses existed on paperback formatting, and that's why indie authors need to take a look at this one. Matthews fills a serious business need.

This course demystifies paperback formatting, and it will save you hours of formatting and hundreds of dollars in formatting costs. I took the course earlier this year, and it is worth the money.

Make Your Paperback Interiors Look Traditionally-Published With These Templates

You've finished formatting your paperback for CreateSpace, and it looks great, but you're worried that it looks a bit plain.

That's the story of my life.

Or at least it was until I found Derek Murphy's DIY Book Formats, a free bundle of CreateSpace templates with flair that rivals that of traditionally published books. Murphy, a highly-acclaimed book cover designer, created these templates as a value-add for his DIY Book Covers service.

DIY Book Formats contains a number of templates for different genres, and you can customize them as you wish. For the most part, they're ready for CreateSpace right out of the box, so you just have to copy and then tweak to your taste (I recommend Jason Matthews's course if you need to tweak them).

I used Murphy's templates this year, and I can't tell you how many compliments I received at an author event when readers visited my table.

And best of all, they're free (at least at the time of this writing)!

Murphy released the templates last year, but he made updates to them this year, which is why they made this year's SOTU.

Writing Craft

There are many writing craft books released every year—some are better than others.

This year authors were blessed with some amazing writing books.

Write Better Faster

Every author wishes they could write faster, but indie author Monica Leonelle makes even the fastest authors look like tortoises.

In her book, *Write Better, Faster: How to Triple Your Writing Speed and Write More Every Day*, she details how she uses outlining, the Pomodoro Method, and dictation to boost her word count from 900 words per hour to 4000 words per hour (no, she's not exaggerating, and yes, you read that correctly!).

At the time of this writing, Monica is on track to release 22 books this year, so her methods work—and they're surprisingly simple.

Write Better Faster is the first book in her Growth Hacking for Storytellers series, which is designed to help indie authors with writing and marketing so that they can be their very best.

How to Write 2 Million Words a Year Every Year Until You Die

Years ago, if you would have pitched me the idea of dictating a novel, I would have run the other way screaming.

But dictation has come a long way, and it was a buzzword this year as more authors discovered how to perfect it for their needs. Dragon Dictation by Nuance is the Scrivener of dictation, and it has helped many authors reach new levels in their writing. Combined with a good microphone, Dragon is extremely accurate.

Many authors I know can write between 500 and 1000 words per hour, which isn't terrible, but it's not incredible, either.

With dictation, however, it is possible to write anywhere from 2,000 to 5,000 words an hour.

Cindy Grigg details her dictation process in her book *The Productive Author's Guide to Dictation: Speak Your Way to Higher (and Healthier!) Word Counts*. She also includes dictation exercises to help you get comfortable with speaking your book.

Chris Fox wrote a similar book called *5000 Words Per Hour: Write Faster, Write Smarter* that covers how he used dictation to hit insane word counts.

Fox also created an iOS app that helps authors keep track of how fast they're actually writing.

And Monica Leonelle released her book *Dictate Your Book: How to Write Your Book Faster, Better, and Smarter*, where she lays out her philosophy of how and why all authors should consider dictation. It's eloquently written and convinced me to take the leap.

All three books are worth reading because they approach the topic from different angles. If you need convincing that dictation is worth it, read Monica's book. If you're sold on the idea but aren't sure how to actually do it, read Grigg. If you're comfortable with the idea but want proof of what is possible, then read Fox (his app is excellent, too). All three of their books complement each other and aren't competitors, in my opinion.

If you still can't wrap your head around dictation, use me as evidence. I dictated this entire book, and I did it in one draft with minimal errors! After professional editing, there was virtually no difference from this book and last year's *State of the Union*, which I typed.

I adopted dictation this year and it tripled my word count while preserving my quality. I'm already a 12-book-a-year writer (and I type fairly slow, around 1000 words an hour). I can't wait to see where I end up next year!

Why Taking Off Your Pants When You Write is the Secret to Success

Are you a pantser or plotter?

Libbie Hawker makes the case for plotting in her book *Take Off Your Pants! Outline Your Book for Faster, Better Writing*.

Hawker helps authors with common outlining problems, and the last paragraph of her book description says it best: "Hawker's outlining technique works no matter what genre you write, and no matter the age of your audience. If you want to improve your writing speed, increase your backlist, and ensure a quality book before you even write the first word, this is the how-to book for you."

I read the book and highly recommend it. Plus the title was hilarious to dictate!

The Stages of a
Fiction Writer

Where are you in your fiction career?

I've often wondered this myself. It would be so nice to have a roadmap of where I've been, where I am, and where I'm going. More often than not, the future isn't clear, no matter how well you plan for it.

According to Dean Wesley Smith, all fiction writers flow through a predictable set of stages. He talks about these stages in great length in his book *Stages of a Fiction Writer*. He writes that beginning authors often focus on words and sentences, while advanced authors focus on story. He offers advice on how to get from one stage to another if you're stuck.

The book is very insightful and there's nothing else like it on the market right now.

This is the Craziest Writing Theory Book You'll Ever Read

What happens when you take an extremely analytical approach to the craft of storytelling?

Professional editor Shawn Coyne explored the idea in his book *The Story Grid: What Good Editors Know*. Coyne, who edited many of Stephen Pressfield's books, describes a framework called the Story Grid that helps authors think about story outlines in terms of story, character, and emotion.

Using *Silence of the Lambs* as an example, Coyne includes an extremely detailed, visual graph that breaks down the story in an almost mathematical way. Authors can use this grid as a starting point to determine if their story is working or not. If it's not working, Coyne provides some tools to fix it.

Right-brained authors will be at home in this book.

Learn Scrivener Really, Really, Really Fast (Seriously!)

Do you still struggle with Scrivener?

With Joseph Michael's *Learn Scrivener Fast* course, you'll never have to struggle again. Joseph did a slew of free webinars this year with notable influencers such as *The Self-Publishing Podcast* and Joanna Penn. He spent an hour in each webinar going over the basics of Scrivener and how to use it like a pro.

I've taken the *Learn Scrivener Fast* course and can't recommend it enough. The investment paid for itself many times over already in terms of the number of hours it saved me. And I was already pretty good at Scrivener before taking the course.

Scrivener's not difficult to learn, but it can be difficult to master if you don't have the right teacher.

Joseph is the right teacher.

The Cutting
Edge of Publishing

One of the important keys to being a successful indie author is being able to look forward and predict where the market is going.

Here are some exciting technologies that will eventually make their way into the mainstream.

Authors Will Hate This New Payment Method, But Readers Will Love It

What if, in the near future, authors' royalty payments were calculated based on how much of a book readers consume?

I am of course referring to the new Kindle Unlimited payout scheme, but a Jerusalem startup company has taken that idea much further.

In an article on *Publishing Perspectives*, Edward Nawotka features Total BooX, which is trying to change the way Millennials read. According to the website, readers can download books on Total BooX for free and are only charged for how much of the book they read.

In discussing Millennial reading habits, Yoav Lorch, the company's CEO, says in Nawotka's article "The idea that there is a ritual to reading[…]is such a rarity today. You're constantly being interrupted. […] The ability to maintain the unwinding experience of reading, the basic experience of narrative fiction and nonfiction, it doesn't happen …"

Total BooX has a catalogue of approximately 40,000 titles. They are not currently open to indie authors unless they have been vetted by professional book review services. The company has an app on iOS and Android.

Takeaway: If the Kindle Unlimited 2.0 change concerns you, you haven't seen anything yet. I don't know if Total BooX will succeed or not, but its business model probably will.

This is the future, folks. The idea that readers can download any book they want for free and only pay for what they read is a sound one, especially as ebook subscription services increase in prominence. It's hard to think that "ownership" of ebooks could decline, but it's possible. Think about all of the ebooks on your ereader/phone. If you're like me, you own hundreds of them. How many of them did you read this year? How many of them did you reread? And when I say reread, I mean reread the entire book from cover to cover.

Exactly.

I see an ecosystem in the future much like Total BooX's. However, ebook ownership won't go away—if readers want to own the book, they'll pay a higher price for it.

Love it or hate it, it's coming. It's a win for readers and a lose for authors (maybe).

Don't be afraid, though. It's not going to be the end of the world. Writing a good, engaging book will remain as important as ever. Focus on doing that and you'll have nothing to worry about.

Virtual Reality and the Future of Publishing

Joanna Penn wrote a guest post at *The Bookseller* exploring the future of virtual reality and the role it might play in publishing.

Penn explores the concept of virtual indie bookstores, where readers can discover new books and interact with booksellers and get recommendations—all from the comfort of their couch. She also explores the financial benefits of VR technology and makes a strong case for the publishing industry to invest in adopting new reading technologies.

She writes "We're not competing against each other, we're competing against gaming and on-demand film/TV as well as music. These industries are embracing VR, and the immersive experience will take consumers even farther from books. We need to embrace this technology and invest in what the online retail environment will be in five years' time."

Is This the Solution to Discoverability?

Porter Anderson covered a new company that believes it has the solution to discoverability.

That company is Trajectory, whose algorithms scan the text of a book and compare plot details, character traits, writing style, and other content-based data points to other books in order to make book recommendations to readers. You can see the algorithm at work by visiting the company's website, which contains a carousel of the books most recently scanned by the algorithm.

Here's how Trajectory differs from Amazon: As far as we know, Amazon does not scan the content of Kindle books in order to make its recommendations. This is why authors have to use metadata in order to tell its search engines what their books are about so that readers can discover them. Because there are only so many searchable, money-making keywords, authors are in fierce competition with each other to grab readers' eyeballs.

Trajectory differs from Amazon and the other ebook retailers because it makes books discoverable based on their content (which Anderson discusses at length in the article). So, in theory, if your book is about pirates, is written at thriller pacing, and contains a plot twist in the book where one of the sidekicks becomes a bad guy, Trajectory would look for other books with those same content similarities. It would compare your data to similar books, down to the very words you use and your sentence lengths, and it would make assumptions based on any connections (or lack thereof) it finds. This is what makes Trajectory so revolutionary.

Trajectory is building its number of books by partnering with retailers and publishing industry associations to develop a robust database of books from which to make its recommendations. They are focusing on scanning traditionally published books right now, but indie authors whose books are tracked with a Bowker ISBN may be eligible to be scanned by the algorithm.

Takeaway: This type of technology really excites me. My article doesn't do it justice; visit the website to see it in action. I would love to be an author in an ecosystem where books are indexed this way. If Trajectory continues on its current trajectory (pun fully intended), I can see an ebook retailer like Amazon or Apple purchasing them. Then the game changes.

In many ways, it would also eliminate a lot of the competition, because authors won't have to compete with each other over limited metadata searches. In theory, a book would only be in competition with books that are similar to it—and as we all know, there's no such thing as competition between authors. If readers like two books, they will probably buy each of those books eventually.

Trajectory takes metadata to a whole new level, and I hope it succeeds. When you compare it to Amazon, you can really see the flaws and weaknesses in Amazon's algorithms, despite the fact that they're currently the best in the world. This just goes to show you that no matter how good something is, it can always be better.

Here's What the Future of Crime Looks Like

In his book, *Future Crimes*, Marc Goodman talks about the pitfalls of an increasingly digital, interconnected world. Goodman, a former law enforcement officer turned security watchdog, talks about some very scary things that cyber criminals are doing on computers, mobile devices, and wireless networks to exploit people online. He also talks about big data companies like Facebook and Google, and what they are doing (and not doing) to solve the problems.

Goodman offers insightful advice on how to protect yourself online and avoid becoming a victim of cyber crime.

Takeaway: While this book does not relate directly to indie authors, it's important because we spend 99% of our time online. We seldom think about the serious exposures we face: For example, you're in a coffee shop writing your book when a hacker exploits the fact that you're using the cafe's free wireless. They use that to access all of the documents on your computer. They install a bad script that locks up your computer screen and threaten to destroy all of your books both on your computer and in the cloud unless you pay then $1,000.00 by midnight.

Or, they find a way to access your personal information and then use that to steal your identity. Anything is possible.

Cyber crime is real, folks. Nothing will stop the momentum of your writing business like getting your identity stolen. As someone who has had his identity stolen, I can tell you that you'll *hate* the time it takes to restore your credibility. That's time better spent writing. So much of being an authorpreneur also involves protecting your business from risks. Just as you would protect yourself from a lawsuit, you should do your best to protect yourself from cyber crime. Everyone should, but indie authors *especially* should.

Cyber crime is only going to get worse, so I can't recommend Goodman's book enough. The section at the end of the book where he outlines exactly how to protect yourself is worth the price of the book ten times over.

*Marketing &
Promotion*

Another great part about the publishing industry is all of the cool products and services that come out every year for indie authors.

2015 was a good year for continuing education. There were a lot of high quality books and services released that will help take your marketing to the next level.

Use Facebook Advertising to Build Your List and Increase Your Sales

If you've written off Facebook as an effective marketing tool, you might want to reconsider.

Bestselling indie author Mark Dawson experimented with Facebook ads and achieved explosive results. Dawson gave numerous interviews this year about his methods, and he unveiled a video course called Self-Publishing Formula that gives indie authors a step-by-step formula to reproduce his success.

Dawson offers three free videos that will teach you the basics of Facebook advertising so you can see the Self-Publishing Formula at work.

Many authors who have taken Dawson's course have raved about it.

How to Generate a Six-Figure Income

Bestselling indie author Nick Stephenson released some great products this year, detailing how he developed a six-figure income from his books. Stephenson wrote a well-received book called Reader Magnets and also gave some fantastic interviews on his success on most of the major self-publishing podcasts.

Your First 10K Readers is a video course designed to teach indie authors how to build a mailing list through compelling calls to action in the back of their books. It also teaches the ins and outs of each specific ebook retailer and how to maximize your metadata for improved visibility.

I took Stephenson's training videos, and about a month after applying his techniques, my sales doubled. His techniques work—at least for me.

Write Better Sales Copy With These Three Tools

Indie authors got a lot of help in writing book descriptions this year.

In her book *Gotta Read It!: Five Simple Steps to a Fiction Pitch That Sells*, Libbie Hawker lays out a simple, step-by-step method for writing fiction product descriptions.

Dean Wesley Smith undertook a massive challenge this year in which he wrote a short story every day in July. He also wrote book descriptions for each story. In his book, his book *How to Write Fiction Sales Copy*, he offers some unique approaches to writing sales copy that I personally have never seen before.

For authors that need professional help, author Bryan Cohen unveiled a new service called Best Page Forward, where he writes product descriptions that sell. The service launched to rave reviews, so much that he launched a premium course called Selling for Authors that also did very well.

Mooberry Dreams: Making Book Pages Dreamy Since 2015

Do you have a "books" page on your author website but hate the way it looks?

Have you tried all of the WordPress author plugins but been disappointed at their lack of flexibility?

Enter the Mooberry Dreams suite of plugins for WordPress, which helps authors create beautiful book pages that balance beauty, functionality, and flexibility.

A Mooberry Dreams book page has the following elements: the book cover in all its glory, logos of the retailers where the book is available, a book description, customizable metadata, an "Add to Goodreads" button, testimonials, and an optional excerpt.

The plugin also supports a grid view so readers can see multiple books in a series.

In my opinion, the greatest feature of the plugin is the retailer logos, sized and formatted for your convenience. I can't tell you what a pain in the neck it is to hunt for ebook retailer images and then format them to play nice on a WordPress page. Not. Fun.

Mooberry Dreams eliminates that hassle.

But what if you want to sell books directly from your site or a site that isn't in Mooberry's default image library? No problem! You can upload a logo and the plugin will format it for you. For books sold directly on my site, I uploaded the Michael La Ronn logo and it links directly to Gumroad. It works brilliantly.

At the time of this writing, the plugin is still new, and its creator, Christie Speith, is constantly making changes to improve its visibility and functionality.

OK, enough chit-chat—are you ready to take your book pages to the next level?

Build a Smarter List
With Author.Email

Authorpreneurs Kevin Tumlinson and Nick Thacker unveiled a new service called Author.email, designed to provide a low-cost, high functionality mailing list solution for authors who want to use mailing lists but don't necessarily want to pay the high prices associated with Aweber or Mailchimp.

Author.email is powered by Amazon Web Services, the same architecture that powers many popular startup websites. The service is free for the first 1,000 subscribers, and has easy-to-use autoresponders that are available to everyone who uses the platform. Tumlinson and Thacker have also promised a simple, clean interface with customizable templates and an easy import process for authors who want to bring their current lists over to the platform.

After the first 1,000 subscribers, the service costs $10 a month. You'll pay only $10/month until you have a list size of 10,000 subscribers (at which point the monthly fee is $20). For a list size of 10,000, MailChimp and Aweber would cost approximately $75 and $149/month, respectively.

Takeaway: I think this is a fantastic idea. Kevin Tumlinson is a friend of mine, but that did not influence my selection of this article. Kevin has a marketing and business background that often gives him a unique insight into the marketplace.

Here's why I like the idea: I talk to authors all the time who tell me that they want to start a mailing list but are discouraged that Mailchimp's free version doesn't come with autoresponders, and AWeber costs at least $200 a year. Right now, the most cost-effective way to get autoresponder functionality is to use Mailchimp's pay as you go plan, which works great but doesn't meet all of an author's needs when they need more sophisticated tools to do things like tracking readers, promoting book launches, starting a street team, etc.

While AWeber is absolutely worth the money, many authors don't have the mailing list volume that justifies the expense yet. Author.email, if it catches hold, could be a great starting point for beginner and midlist authors just starting their lists, giving them high quality tools while they build their platforms.

Action Items for All Indie Authors in 2016

Every year, something happens that requires authors to make some changes to their business operations in order to continue with business as usual.

You'll need to take immediate action on the items in this section in order to avoid potential issues, so take them seriously!

Why Your Credit Card Reader Is No Longer Valid

Do you have a credit card reader?

If your card reader can't read chip technology, stop using it immediately.

Effective October 1, 2015, credit card companies have instituted new policies that affect business owners everywhere. It's called the EMV Liability Shift (EMV stands for Europay, MasterCard and Visa).

Under the shift, if you use a regular card reader to accept payment from a chip credit card and that transaction is fraudulent, then you will be liable. You will need an EMV card reader in order to properly read chip cards. Square offers a new EMV card reader, and other companies are also following suit.

In light of the record credit card fraud around the world, credit card companies have invested in chip and pin technology in order to cut down on fraud. Chip cards are safer and offer greater protection if your credit card is ever stolen. If you bank with a major credit card company, you may already have one of these cards. You may have also noticed that big retailers have already equipped their cash registers with new card readers.

Since credit card companies have spent their time, effort and money creating a new technology, they're going to have zero-tolerance for merchants who don't jump onboard. Merchants who fail to adopt the new technology will leave themselves open to potential fines and lawsuits.

Do not accept ANY credit card payments at your next author event without an EMV-compliant card reader.

Square offers a brand new, EMV-compliant card reader for as little as $49. Be a good business owner and buy one right now if you haven't already.

VATMOSS: The New Euro Tax Law and Why It's Eating Into Your Sales

The European Union passed tax reform legislation in 2015 that will affect the entire publishing industry.

The law is called the Value-Added Tax Mini One Stop Shopping (VATMOSS), and it governs how business owners collect taxes from customers.

Before VATMOSS, goods were taxed based on the seller's country. For example, if you live in Germany but buy a book from a Dutch author, the Dutch author's tax rates applied to the sale.

VATMOSS mandates that business owners have to collect taxes based on where the customer is located at the time of the sale. So, in the scenario above, the German customer's tax rates would apply, and it would be the Dutch author's responsibility to figure out where the German was located at the time of sale so that he could calculate the right tax rate. If the German author is on holiday in Spain when he buys the book, Spain's tax rates would apply.

Business owners across the European Union opposed the law because it's difficult to know where a customer is at any given point of time. To implement the proper tracking mechanisms is expensive and prohibitive for small businesses.

Amazon and all the ebook retailers changed their policies in response to the law. Book prices are now VAT-inclusive, which means that if you price your book at €9.99, the VAT tax will come out of the €9.99 first, then Amazon's cut, and *then* your royalty. The VAT is different for every country and is complicated because it uses a tier system based on a number of factors.

You'll either have to adjust the Euro prices of your books upward to make up for the new tax rate, or absorb it and take a hit on your royalties. Difficult decision.

But whatever you do, you need to go to all your ebook retailers and adjust the price of your book in Euros.

If you're selling books through the ebook retailers or direct on your site through Gumroad or another third-party service, all you have to do is adjust your prices at this time.

However, if you're accepting direct payments from customers, you're in for a headache. Do your research and figure out how to mitigate your tax liability, as there are strict penalties for businesses that don't comply with the law.

Japanese Consumption Tax: Why You Need to Adjust Your Japanese Book Prices

Effective October 1, 2015, Japan implemented a law similar in spirit to the VATMOSS, implementing a consumption tax for all ebooks.

The new Japanese consumption tax is 8% and is inclusive. Some retailers like Amazon and Kobo have minimum pricing requirements for Yen, so it's important that you do the calculation to know how much your royalties will be impacted.

You need to adjust your book prices in Yen as soon as possible. Note that Amazon pays a 70% royalty for Japanese sales only if you're in KDP Select; if you're not exclusive the royalty drops down to 35%.

The real takeaway here is that it's probably a good time to evaluate the price of your book in all currencies. You should be doing this manually (don't let the ebook retailers calculate it for you).

Study the pricing articles I mentioned earlier in this book, and spend some time on international versions of the big ebook retailers to see how other authors are pricing their books. Make sure your book's price fits with the genre and competition. Just because your book is priced at $4.99 in the United States doesn't mean that the equivalent of $4.99 will work in India.

The last thing you want to do is lose out on sales because you didn't do your homework.

Update Your Website or Google Will Murder It

Google announced a major update to its Google Search engine that will affect indie authors.

Due to the increased number of mobile readers, Google will now rank websites that are optimized for mobile reading higher than those that are not.

Mobile-friendly sites will be marked with a "mobile-friendly" label that will appear prominently in web searches.

According to Google, a mobile-friendly website does the following:

* avoids software that is not common on mobile devices, like Flash

* uses text that is readable without zooming

* sizes content to the screen so users don't have to scroll horizontally or zoom

* places links far enough apart so that the correct one can be easily tapped

Google offers a Mobile-Friendly Test tool so you can test your website and see what needs to be fixed. Most authors I spoke to have reported that making updates is relatively simple because many website themes and plugins are also updating to be in compliance with Google's SEO requirements.

I updated my site earlier this year; because I was using a premium WordPress theme, I only had to make some minor updates. It took about an hour or so, but that's because I'm familiar with WordPress.

Suffice to say that it's a smart idea to comply with Google's guidelines, or it will make your website harder to be discovered by readers who are looking for you.

Elance and Odesk Are Now Upwork

Many authors have used Elance and Odesk to find freelancers such as cover designers and editors to work on their books. Both are the largest freelancing sites in the world.

Elance and Odesk merged in 2013. In 2015, they announced that both of the services would be going away and replaced by Upwork, a single platform with essentially the same functionality but with an improved look and some other updates that Elance and Odesk both needed.

If you haven't done so already, it's a good idea to start your profile to Upwork if you want to continue using this ecosystem. Also make sure to confirm that any freelancers you normally do business with will also be migrating over to Upwork. Be sure to get their email addresses just in case you cannot contact them for any reason.

However, heed this friendly warning: Read the Elance/Odesk and Upwork terms of service. If you were working with a freelancer on Elance previously and want to just work directly via PayPal, it may be a violation of the company's exclusivity clause. I don't recommend it. You are required to use Upwork/Elance/Odesk exclusively for 48 months with any freelancer that you find on the platform (99Designs has a similar exclusivity clause). If you try to move your relationship off the platform, it could be a violation of the terms of service. And from what I've heard, Upwork takes these violations just as seriously as Amazon takes KDP Select violations (read:

don't piss them off).

Terms of service and exclusivity aside, Upwork is a sleek platform. There are numerous benefits to using it instead of working directly with a freelancer. It protects both you and the freelancer in the event of a dispute or fraud. It also does the heavy lifting at tax time by sending out 1099s for you, which is extremely helpful for indie authors who can't afford tax software.

Subscribe to the Author Level Up YouTube Channel

So the last action item is the easiest of all.

As I mentioned in the beginning of the book, I have started a YouTube channel called Author Level Up. I create weekly videos that help authors take their career to the next level.

On Thursdays, I do writing craft videos to help you write better stories faster.

On Fridays, I do business & marketing videos to help you become a smarter authorpreneur.

On Saturdays, I talk about the major publishing industry news of the week and the implications that it will have on us as authors. Think of it like an Indie Author State of the Union every week.

Most of my videos are five minutes or less, and I promise that you'll find them helpful and informative. And quirky.

You can also submit questions to the channel and if I can, I'll make a video response that answers your question in great detail.

Video is next big frontier for authors. Few are using it, so this will be a fun adventure for me to see what works!

You can learn more about the channel at www.authorlevelup.com.

Predictions for 2016

When I made my predictions last year, they seemed natural. Amazon will revamp Kindle Unlimited? Check. Apple will position itself to be a competitor? Check.

This year, the future seems more uncertain. A lot of things happened this year that made me double-check the accuracy of my Nostradamus hat.

But the best part about making predictions is that I don't have to be right (just like Nostradamus!)

Based on the trends I've seen in 2015, here are my predictions for 2016:

1. Traditional publishers will finally "get it." They're going to scramble to reclaim their lost market share. It wouldn't surprise me if one of the Big Five jumped into Kindle Unlimited in some form or fashion. If you think competition and discoverability was hard this year, just wait.

2. Kindle Unlimited payouts will continue to decrease and more authors will wrestle publicly with the exclusivity paradox. However, Kindle Unlimited will continue record-setting success. We may start to see even more changes in the Amazon algorithm as a result.

3. More authors will finally "get" the need to be business people. The most experienced of these authors will hunt for information ravenously and find that there isn't much available. The market for practical, skill-based author business books will explode. Authors will need Business 101 lessons specifically tailored to them instead of relying on generic business books and podcasts. Authors, podcasters, and course creators will make very good money catering to this growing market.

4. Podcasting is still wide open for those willing to try it, and video is the next frontier. There is still room for author business podcasts, and I think we'll see a really good one pop up this year. I'm also making play on video for authors being a viable strategy for building an audience (through my Author Level Up YouTube channel).

5. Dictation isn't going away. Expect authors to keep talking about it, and expect to hear more success stories.

6. Competition between Amazon and Apple will heat up. Nook isn't going anywhere. Kobo will continue to grow. D2D will continue to supplant Smashwords's share of the distributor market, and Google will make a decision on whether it will continue or shutter the Play Store for authors.

7. Scrivener will finally get an iOS version and a much-needed update to its desktop version that will make it easier to produce higher quality books. It's long overdue.

8. Audiobooks will still be a safe bet. Sales will continue to grow.

9. Foreign translations haven't panned out the way we thought they would (yet), so you'll see fewer authors talking about them (myself included).

10. An indie author will sign a groundbreaking deal that will get them into libraries, much like Jamie McGuire's Walmart deal this year. Libraries are already the next battleground.

11. The Authors Guild will continue on its misadventures against Amazon, but it will probably be successful in getting publishers to adopt fairer contract terms in lieu of their shrinking market share.

We'll see how the industry unfolds.

But no matter what happens, don't bank your career on hope. Here's a bleak prediction for you: Despite all these wonderful new developments in the industry, despite all the books, podcasts, courses, blog posts, and author conferences that practically ooze useful information, many indie authors won't use them to their advantage. They will just keep on doing what they're doing, and they'll blame everyone but themselves when their careers crash. You may think I'm being harsh, but try running a consulting business for authors sometime and see what kind of personalities you encounter.

The truth is that only a small percentage of authors are willing to truly devote themselves to learning the ins and out of this industry. Sad, but true. And as the next few years go by, we'll start to see many of them dip out of the industry or race to catch up because they didn't stay on top of current developments.

I feel sorry for those authors.

But I don't feel sorry for you. Just by buying this book, you've proven that you're willing to invest in your career. If you keep investing in yourself, you won't stagnate and you won't disappear.

Here's what you can do to further ensure your future success: Write more books and create good products, work on your business, and keep connecting with readers.

Don't chase trends. Don't make decisions out of desperation because your book sales are shrinking. Don't do "hope marketing." Don't let someone convince you that the sky is falling because of some change Amazon made to Kindle Unlimited or some other silliness.

That's a lot of don'ts, but I can back them up with evidence—everything in this book. What you've read in these pages is continued proof that this is the greatest time in the history of the world to be an author. I can't think of another creative industry whose members produce so much helpful information—and who don't constantly try to one-up each other. The indie author community is so incredibly generous. Authors don't have to share their time or their secrets for success, but they do. And we're all better because of it.

No matter how difficult your situation may seem, remember that there is always someone out there who has been through what you're experiencing, and they're probably willing to help.

If you follow the steps above and stay tough, you'll weather whatever changes happen between next year and the end of time.

You might even wake up one morning and find that your dreams have already come true.

See you next year.

--Michael La Ronn
Des Moines, Iowa
December 2, 2015

Thanks for Reading!

Thanks for reading this book. I have two things to ask.

The first is that I now have a YouTube channel called Author Level Up. Basically, it's like the *Indie Author State of the Union* every week. I do writing craft, business, and marketing videos that will help take your career to the next level.

The second is to join my email list (I know, I know—how many times have you heard *that* one before?). But if you enjoyed this video, I also have a ton of emails and free video training that you won't be able to get anywhere else. So come on, you know you want to sign up!

Learn more at www.authorlevelup.com.

Acknowledgments

Cover Design: Pixelstudio
Editing: Calee Allen
Beta readers: Patrick Stemp

And special thanks as always to my wife, daughter, family, and my readers, who make all of this possible for me every day.

Sources

AUTHOR LEVEL UP YOUTUBE CHANNEL

www.authorlevelup.com

BOOK RETAILERS

AMAZON

Amazon Spills the Beans

"Kindle Head Russ Grandinetti Offers View from Amazon at Digital Book World 2015," Digital Book World, January 14, 2015, http://www.digitalbookworld.com/2015/kindle-head-russ-grandinetti-offers-the-view-from-amazon-at-digital-book-world-2015/

"TKC Episode 360 Russ Grandinetti," The Kindle Chronicles Podcast, June 26, 2015, http://www.thekindlechronicles.com/2015/06/26/tkc-360-russ-grandinetti/

New Review Features

"Amazon Adds New Review Features Via Drop Down Menus," Henry Baum, Self-Publishing Review, March 22, 2015, http://www.selfpublishingreview.com/2015/03/amazon-adds-new-review-options-via-drop-down-menus/

Series Pages

Dragon Blood series by Lindsay Buroker, http://www.michaellaronn.com/dragonblood

Ted Saves the World series by Bryan Cohen, http://www.michaellaronn.com/tedsavestheworld

The Fitz and the Fool trilogy by Robin Hobb, http://www.michaellaronn.com/fitzandthefool

KDP EDU

"Amazon Launches Kindle Textbook Creator," Amazon Media Room, January 22, 2015, http://www.michaellaronn.com/kdpedu

Amazon Advertising

"Advertising for KDP Select," Amazon KDP Support Forums, June 2015, http://www.michaellaronn.com/amazonmarketingservices

Amazon Giveaways

"Introducing Amazon Giveaway—The First Self-Service Giveaway Tool," Amazon Media Room, February 10, 2015, http://www.michaellaronn.com/amazongiveaway

European Union Woes

"Antitrust: Commission opens formal investigation into Amazon's e-book distribution arrangements," European Commission Press Release Database, June 11, 2015, http://europa.eu/rapid/press-release_IP-15-5166_en.htm

Kindle Unlimited 2.0

"New Change in Amazon Kindle Unlimited (KU) and KOLL," Amazon KDP Support Forums, June 2015, http://www.michaellaronn.com/ku2

"Kindle Unlimited Scores a Knockout," Hugh Howey, August 15, 2015, http://www.hughhowey.com/kindle-unlimited-knockout/

"Konrath Kindle Unlimited Numbers," Joe Konrath, August 15, 2015, http://jakonrath.blogspot.com/2015/08/konrath-kindle-unlimited-numbers.html

NOOK

"Sears Canada Head to Run Barnes & Noble," Jim Milliot, Publishers Weekly, July 2, 2015, http://www.publishersweekly.com/pw/by-topic/industry-news/people/article/67375-sears-canada-head-to-run-barnes-noble.html

"The Beginning of the End: B&N Shutters the International Nook Store," Nate Hoffelder, Digital Book World, July 8, 2015, http://the-digital-reader.com/2015/07/08/the-beginning-of-the-end-bn-shutters-the-international-nook-store/

Nook Press Print On-Demand: http://www.michaellaronn.com/nookpress

"Barnes & Noble's Dirty Little Secret: Author Solutions and Nook Press," David Gaughran, March 3, 2015, https://davidgaughran.wordpress.com/2015/03/03/barnes-nobles-dirty-little-secret-author-solutions-and-nook-press/

APPLE iBOOKS

"Moerer: iBooks Averages 1 Million New Customers Per Week," Digital Book World, January 15, 2015, http://lunch.publishersmarketplace.com/2015/01/moerer-ibooks-averages-1-million-new-customers-per-week-post-ios8/

"Author ePubs Created with iBooks Author," Apple website, June 29, 2015, http://www.michaellaronn.com/ibooksauthor

"158: Selling Big on Apple with Julia Kent," Self Publishing Podcast, May 20, 2015, http://selfpublishingpodcast.com/self-publishing-podcast-158-how-to-sell-big-on-apple-ibooks-with-julia-kent/

KOBO

"Author Services: Exciting Developments in the Works," Kobo Writing Life blog, August 24, 2015, http://www.michaellaronn.com/kwlauthorservices

"Publishers Weekly 50% Off for KWL Authors," Kobo Writing Life blog, May 28, 2015, http://www.michaellaronn.com/kwlpw

"OverDrive Announces Agreement for Acquisition by Rakuten," OverDrive corporate website, March 19, 2015, http://www.michaellaronn.com/overdrive

SMASHWORDS

"What Indie Authors Need to Know in 2015," Indie reCon interview with Orna Ross, April 15, 2015, http://indierecon.org/what-authors-need-to-know-now-2015-mark-coker-orna-ross/

"State of the Indie Nation with Mark Coker," The Creative Penn podcast, September 7, 2015, http://www.thecreativepenn.com/2015/09/07/indie-nation-mark-coker/

"Smashwords Introduces Assetless Preorders" (aka "Metadata Only" preorders), Smashwords blog, June 17, 2015, http://www.michaellaronn.com/smashwordspreorders

"Smashwords and Flipkart to End Distribution Relationship: Amazon Scores Victory," Mark Coker, Smashwords blog, August 25, 2015, http://www.michaellaronn.com/smashwordsflipkart

"Self-Publishing with Smashwords," Jason Matthews course on Udemy, https://www.udemy.com/self-publishing-with-smashwords/

DRAFT2DIGITAL

"Episode 160: Multi-Platform Distribution with Draft2Digital's Dan Wood," Self Publishing Podcast interview with Johnny B. Truant, Sean Platt, and Dave Wright, June 3, 2015, http://selfpublishingpodcast.com/160-distribution-with-draft2digitals-dan-wood/

"Draft2Digital and Tolino Join Forces," The Passive Voice, January 27, 2015, http://www.thepassivevoice.com/01/2015/draft2digital-and-tolino-join-forces/ [Author's note: Due to the redesign of the Draft2Digital website, the original press release was no longer available when I wrote this book, so I went with the most neutral, passive source I could find that had an excerpt of the press release in it].

"Author-Favorite Ebook Distributor Partners with Leading Ebook Subscription Service," Draft2Digital website, June 25, 2015, http://www.michaellaronn.com/d2doyster

"Feature Highlight - Automated End Matter," Draft2Digital website, October 2015, https://draft2digital.com/blog/feature-highlight-end-matter/

"Feature Highlight - New Release Notifications," Draft2Digital website, November 2015, https://draft2digital.com/blog/feature-highlight-new-release-notifications/

Books2Read website: www.books2read.com

GOOGLE PLAY

"Google Play Becomes the 9th Android App Installed on Over 1 Billion Devices," Bertel King, Jr., Android Police, June 8, 2015, http://www.androidpolice.com/2015/06/08/google-play-books-becomes-the-9th-android-app-installed-on-over-1-billion-devices/

"Google Play Shutters Its Play Books Publishers Portal in Order to 'Improve Content Management Capabilities,'" Nate Hoffelder, The Digital Reader, May 25, 2015, http://the-digital-reader.com/2015/05/25/google-shutters-its-play-books-publisher-portal-in-order-to-improve-its-content-management-capabilities/

OYSTER AND SCRIBD

"Macmillan US Joins Oyster and Scribd," Lisa Campbell, The Bookseller, January 13, 2015, http://www.thebookseller.com/news/macmillan-us-joins-oyster-and-scribd

"Eyeing Amazon, Oyster Launches ebookstore with All Big Five Publishers," Digital Book World, April 8, 2015, http://www.digitalbookworld.com/2015/eyeing-amazon-oyster-launches-ebookstore-with-all-big-five-publishers/ [Original press release was not available at time of writing]

"Oyster Shucks Its Streaming Ebook Service," Nate Hoffelder, The Digital Reader, September 21, 2015, http://the-digital-reader.com/2015/09/21/oyster-shucks-its-streaming-ebook-service/

"Scribd Adds Unlimited Comic Books to Its Subscription Service," Trevor Courneen, Paste Magazine (via Scribd.com), February 10, 2015, http://www.pastemagazine.com/articles/2015/02/scribd-adds-unlimited-comic-books-to-its-subscript.html

"Is the Subscription Model in Trouble? Scribd Dumps Romance Titles," Bob Mayer, June 30, 2015, https://writeitforward.wordpress.com/2015/06/30/is-the-subscription-model-in-trouble-scribd-dumps-romance-titles/

"A Message from Our CEO," Trip Adler, Scribd website, August 21, 2015, http://www.michaellaronn.com/scribdaudiobooks

"Scribd Cuts Romance Catalogue," Mark Coker, Smashwords blog, June 30, 2015, http://www.teleread.com/book-subscription-services/scribd-to-cut-romance-and-erotica-titles-from-its-catalog/

TRADITIONAL PUBLISHING

"E-Book Sales Fall After Amazon Contracts," Jeffrey A. Trachtenberg, The Wall Street Journal, September 3, 2015, http://www.wsj.com/article_email/e-book-sales-weaken-amid-higher-prices-1441307826-lMyQjAxMTE1MzAxNDUwMjQ2Wj [Link may expire]

"Shocking WSJ Discovery: Higher Prices=Lower Volume!" Joe Konrath, September 4, 2015, http://jakonrath.blogspot.com/2015/09/shocking-wsj-discovery-higher.html

"Author Solutions and Friends: The Inside Story," David Gaughran, April 29, 2015, https://davidgaughran.wordpress.com/2015/04/29/author-solutions-and-friends-the-inside-story-2/

"The Real Price of Traditional Publishing," Dean Wesley Smith, June 22, 2015, http://www.deanwesleysmith.com/the-new-world-of-publishing-the-real-price-of-traditional-publishing/

LIBRARIES

"Cautions on E-Books," Daniel Goldstein, Inside Higher Ed, February 6, 2015, https://www.insidehighered.com/views/2015/02/06/essay-problems-economic-model-e-books-poses-college-libraries-and-scholars

"Douglas Counties Library Report," Douglas County Libraries, March 2, 2015, http://americanlibrariesmagazine.org/wpcontent/uploads/2015/03/DCLPricingComparison030215.pdf

"Ebooks for Libraries," Joe Konrath, March 26, 2015, http://jakonrath.blogspot.com/2015/03/ebooks-for-libraries.html

Ebooks Are Forever website: http://www.ebooksareforever.com

"How Self-Published Authors Can Distribute to Libraries," Porter Anderson, Jane Friedman's blog, July 2, 2015, https://janefriedman.com/selfpub-distribution-libraries/

Self-e Website: http://self-e.libraryjournal.com/

INTERNATIONAL MARKETS

Global Ebook Report: http://www.global-ebook.com/

"Amazon Announces Second Annual Indie Literary Prize for Spanish-Language Authors," Amazon Media Room, May 12, 2015, www.michaellaronn.com/spanishliteraryprize

"Kobo Announces Partnership with Mexico's Top Book Retailers," Kobo Writing Life Blog, July 28, 2015, http://www.michaellaronn.com/kobomexico

"Opportunities in Mexico for Digital Growth," Digital Book World, August 27th, 2015, http://www.digitalbookworld.com/2015/opportunities-in-mexico-for-digital-growth/

"Will Europe's New E-commerce Tax Lead to Digital Disenfranchisement?" Stuart Lauchlan, Diginomica, November 12, 2014, http://diginomica.com/2014/11/12/will-europes-new-ecommerce-tax-lead-digital-disenfranchisement/#.VfMcSxFVhBe

"EU Court Rules E-Books are Services, Not Goods," Valentina Pop, The Wall Street Journal, March 5, 2015, http://www.wsj.com/article_email/eu-court-rules-e-books-are-services-not-goods-1425552050-lMyQjAxMTE1NjA4NTYwNTU0Wj [article link may expire]

Helpful flowchart to understand the VATMOSS laws: https://www.gov.uk/government/publications/vat-supplying-digital-services-to-private-consumers

"Kindle Unlimited Ruled Illegal in France," Nate Hoffelder, The Digital Reader, February 15, 2015, http://the-digital-reader.com/2015/02/19/kindle-unlimited-ruled-illegal-in-france/

"German Ebook Sales Reach 4.3% of Overall Market," Ingrid Süßmann, Publishing Perspectives, June 24, 2015, http://publishingperspectives.com/2015/06/german-ebook-sales-reaches-4-3-of-overall-book-market/

"In Germany: Ebooks Less than 10% of Market, Tolino Grows," Edward Nawotka, Publishing Perspectives, February 27, 2015, http://publishingperspectives.com/2015/02/in-germany-ebooks-less-than-10-of-market-tolino-grows/

"E-books overtake paper in China," Xinhuanet, April 20, 2015, http://news.xinhuanet.com/english/2015-04/20/c_134167260.htm

"Selling Ebooks in China," Patrick Crowley, Vearsa website, March 30, 2015, https://www.vearsa.com/selling-ebooks-in-china/

BUSINESS

"The Definitive Guide to Pricing Your Book," Wise Ink Blog, April 14, 2015, http://www.wiseinkblog.com/self-publishing-2/the-definitive-guide-to-pricing-your-book/

"8 Psychological Triggers to Optimize Your Product Page," Kiss Metrics blog, Talia Wolf, December 2014, https://blog.kissmetrics.com/pricing-page-psychological-triggers/

"Broken, Not Bitter: An Author's Life with Repetitive Stress Injuries," Marianne Sciucco, guest post on The Creative Penn, August 20, 2015, http://www.thecreativepenn.com/2015/08/20/repetitive-strain-injury-rsi/

"How a Book Becomes a Movie," Jane Friedman, July 27, 2015, https://janefriedman.com/how-a-book-becomes-a-movie/

"How to Sell Your Screenplay (for Absolute Beginners)," Jane Friedman, June 16, 2015, https://janefriedman.com/how-to-sell-your-screenplay/

Mock Publishing Contract Forms by IP attorney Daniel N. Steven: http://publishlawyer.com/forms/

Indie Recon 2015: http://indierecon.org/

"January Author Earnings Report," Hugh Howey and Data Guy, January 18, 2015, http://authorearnings.com/report/january-2015-author-earnings-report/

"May Author Earnings Report," Hugh Howey and Data Guy, May 6, 2015, http://authorearnings.com/report/may-2015-author-earnings-report/

"September Author Earnings Report," Hugh Howey and Data Guy, September 14, 2015, http://authorearnings.com/report/september-2015-author-earnings-report/

October Author Earnings Report," Hugh Howey and Data Guy, October 9, 2015, http://authorearnings.com/report/october-2015-apple-bn-kobo-and-google-a-look-at-the-rest-of-the-ebook-market/

2015 Writer's Tax Workshop by E.M. Lynley: http://www.michaellaronn.com/2015taxes

The Write Attitude by Kristine Kathryn Rusch: http://www.michaellaronn.com/attitudeforwriters

Playing the Short Game by Douglas Smith: http://www.michaellaronn.com/playingtheshortgame

Prosperity for Writers by Honoree Corder: http://www.michaellaronn.com/prosperity

CreateSpace & Kindle Author Business Plans Made Easy by Ryan Petty: http://www.michaellaronn.com/businessplans

Indie Poet Rock Star series by Michael La Ronn: http://www.michaellaronn.com/thefutureofpoetry

WRITING CRAFT

The Productive Author's Guide to Dictation by Cindy Grigg: http://www.michaellaronn.com/productivedictation

5000 Words Per Hour by Chris Fox: http://www.michaellaronn.com/5000wph

Dictate Your Book by Monica Leonelle: http://www.michaellaronn.com/dictateyourbook

Recommended Software & Hardware for Dictation: http://www.michaellaronn.com/dictationsetup

Take Off Your Pants by Libbie Hawker: http://www.michaellaronn.com/takeoffyourpants

Stages of a Fiction Writer by Dean Wesley Smith: http://www.deanwesleysmith.com/

The Story Grid by Shawn Coyne: http://www.michaellaronn.com/storygrid

Learn Scrivener Fast course by Joseph Michael: http://learnscrivenerfast.com/

MARKETING

Self-Publishing Formula course by Mark Dawson: http://www.selfpublishingformula.com/

Your First 10K Readers course by Nick Stephenson: http://www.yourfirst10kreaders.com/

Gotta Read It! By Libbie Hawker and How to Write Fiction Sales Copy by Dean Wesley Smith: http://www.michaellaronn.com/salescopy

Best Page Forward by Bryan Cohen: http://www.bryancohen.com/best-page-forward

Mooberry Dreams WordPress Plugin: http://www.mooberrydreams.com

Author.email: http://www.author.email

LEGAL STUFF

"My Gravity Lawsuit and How It Affects Every Author Who Sells to Hollywood," Tess Gerritsen, January 31, 2015, http://www.tessgerritsen.com/gravity-lawsuit-affects-every-writer-sells-hollywood/

"Gravity Lawsuit Update," Tess Gerritsen, June 15, 2015, http://www.tessgerritsen.com/gravity-lawsuit-update-2/

"In Which I Review My Own Book for Potential Legal Issues," Marc Whipple, April 2015, http://legalinspiration.com/?p=23

My Mother Had Me Tested! by Marc Whipple: http://www.michaellaronn.com/mymother

The Copyright Handbook by Stephen Fishman: http://www.michaellaronn.com/copyright

"Who Owns Your Digital Afterlife?" Matt O'Brien, Mercury News, August 28, 2015, http://www.mercurynews.com/business/ci_28721510/who-owns-your-digital-afterlife

Kristine Kathryn Rusch's Estate Planning blog series: http://kriswrites.com/business-rusch-publishing-articles/estate-planning-series/

"What Happens When an Author Dies. Estate Planning with Kathryn Goldman." Joanna Penn, The Creative Penn, November 23, 2015, http://www.thecreativepenn.com/2015/11/23/estate-planning-kathryn-goldman/

COVER DESIGN & BOOK FORMATTING

"Jungle Book: Simple Kindle Book Analysis," Jason van Gamester, The Digital Reader, August 31, 2015, http://the-digital-reader.com/2015/08/31/junglebook-simple-kindle-ebook-cover-analysis/

"The Kindle Finally Gets Typography That Doesn't Suck," John Brownlee, Fast Company, May 27, 2015, http://www.fastcodesign.com/3046678/the-kindle-finally-gets-typography-that-doesnt-suck

"Google announces Literata, its new ebook typeface," Nate Swanner, The Next Web, May 18, 2015, http://thenextweb.com/google/2015/05/18/google-announces-literata-its-new-e-book-typeface/

"Calibre Convert to Epub," course by Jason Matthews on UDemy: https://www.udemy.com/calibre-convert-to-epub-file/

"Make Paperbacks with CreateSpace: Sell More Books on Amazon," course by Jason Matthews on UDemy: https://www.udemy.com/make-paperbacks-with-createspace-sell-more-books-on-amazon/

DIY Book Formats by Derek Murphy: http://www.diybookformats.com/ DIY Book Formats instantly

DIY Book Covers by Derek Murphy: http://diybookcovers.com/

THE CUTTING EDGE

"Total BooX: E-Books for the Way the 21st Century Reader Reads," Edward Nawotka, Publishing Perspectives, March 13, 2015, http://publishingperspectives.com/2015/03/total-boox-ebooks-for-the-way-the-21st-century-reader-reads/

Total BooX: http://www.totalboox.com

"Joanna Penn: Virtual reality and the future of publishing," Joanna Penn, The Bookseller, March 16, 2015, http://www.thebookseller.com/futurebook/joanna-penn-virtual-reality-and-future-publishing

"A New Architecture of Algorithms: Could Trajectory Make Books 'Discoverable' At Last?" Porter Anderson, Thought Catalog, January 10, 2015, http://thoughtcatalog.com/porter-anderson/2015/01/a-new-architecture-of-algorithms-could-trajectory-make-books-discoverable-at-last/

Trajectory: http://www.trajectory.com

Future Crimes Book: http://www.futurecrimesbook.com/

ACTION ITEMS

VATMOSS

"Will Europe's New E-commerce Tax Lead to Digital Disenfranchisement?" Stuart Lauchlan, Diginomica, November 12, 2014, http://diginomica.com/2014/11/12/will-europes-new-ecommerce-tax-lead-digital-disenfranchisement/#.VfMcSxFVhBe

Japanese Consumption Tax

"Japan Consumption Tax Will Start October 1, 2015," Kobo Writing Life blog, September 7, 2015, http://www.michaellaronn.com/kobojapan

Google Updates

"Helping Users Find Mobile-Friendly Pages," Google Webmaster Central Blog, November 14, 2014, http://googlewebmastercentral.blogspot.com/2014/11/helping-users-find-mobile-friendly-pages.html

Google Mobile-Friendly Test: https://www.google.com/webmasters/tools/mobile-friendly/

EMV Liability Shift
Square EMV Card Reader: https://squareup.com/emv-liability-shift

About Michael La Ronn

Michael La Ronn is an author, poet, public speaker, and entrepreneur. He writes fearless fantasy and Decision Select Novels, and he is known for his quirky, imaginative writing style. He also writes nonfiction about writing and indie publishing.

In 2012, a life-threatening illness put him in the hospital. Realizing that life was too short, he devoted himself to self-publishing, entrepreneurship, and all the other punishments that indie authors love to bring upon themselves. And he loves every moment of it.

You can connect with Michael at www.authorlevelup.com

Other Books by

Michael La Ronn

Android X (Series)
Eaten (Series)
Festival of Shadows
How to Be Bad
Reconciled People: Stories
Callback from the Muse: Poems
Indie Poet Rock Star (series)
Indie Author State of the Union (series)
Interactive Fiction

www.ingramcontent.com/pod-product-compliance
Lightning Source LLC
Chambersburg PA
CBHW020414300526
45786CB00016B/2209